Endorsements

If you feel like your past is keeping you from what God has for you in your future, Sally Livingston's book *Get OVER it!* will help you break free from what was and help you walk into what could be. This is a must-read for everyone. Eternally grateful for this book.

— Luke Lezon, author, *Your Mess Matters*

If you feel like your relationships or experiences have you stuck in quicksand with no way out - *Get OVER It!* offers a lifeline of hope.

— Kary Oberbrunner, author of *Day Job to Dream Job* and *Your Secret Name*

If you have had a difficult past, as I did, Sally Livingston's book, *Get OVER It!*, is the key that unlocks a new-found freedom!

— Marabel Morgan, author, *The Total Woman*, and memoir, *Hard Beginning, Happy Ending*

I am forever grateful to have been a client of Sally Livingston's. The four-step plan works! This book is a must-read for anyone who wants to love well, be free to dream, and move past fear!

— Debra Petersen- CRU Women's Resources, Women of Faith Speaker Team, Radio Talk Show Host

Life can sometimes feel like the "spin cycle" on your washing machine—it is moving fast but we end up right back where we started. It leaves us feeling stuck, exhausted and discouraged. Sally Livingston's book *Get OVER It!* can help us actually break free from the "spin cycle". She brings a wonderful blend of counseling experience, biblical knowledge, and practical application. This book can help you get the breakthrough you have been longing for.

— Lance Witt, author of *Replenish* and *High Impact Teams*, Founder of Replenish Ministries

In our society today, we are seeing an approach to the difficult and perhaps even traumatic experiences of our lives as something we must live in forever. When one has suffered or struggled, the idea of seeing oneself as a victim for life can be encouraged and expected. For Christians, there is often little distinction from the world concerning how personal life experiences are handled. Is this what God intended for us? For far too many, we find ourselves stuck, rather than living the abundant life that Jesus promised to his people. I am thankful that Sally Livingston has written this timely book that I believe the church needs more than ever. Sally provides a combination of biblical truth, years of experience as a trusted therapist and counselor, and transparency in her words. I believe this combination will help us all be very mindful of the experiences of our lives, without letting them define us as people. Thank you, Sally Livingston for giving us a pathway to *"get over it!"* I recommend Sally's insights, wisdom, counsel, and compassionate teaching found in this new book. I will be sharing it with others!

— Dean Inserra, Pastor, City Church Tallahassee, author of *The Unsaved Christian: Reaching Cultural Christianity with the Gospel*

Sometimes we spend so much time looking backward, we have no idea how to move forward. Sally Livingston's *Get OVER It!* will have you moving forward with confidence, peace & passion. A must-read!

— Noah Herrin, Young Adults Pastor – The Gathering

"It's crazy how sometimes we can repeat behaviors without even noticing their toxicity until it's too late and we're stuck! Sally's practical and biblical wisdom on *getting over* hurts, doubts, and fear is challenging, encouraging, and hopeful. Freedom from your "it" is POSSIBLE!"

— Gracie Parker Bell, Social Media Director, Elevation Worship at Elevation Church

Get OVER It!

FOUR STEPS TO BREAKING FREE FROM THE STUCK CYCLE

— Ken & Donelle
love you so much!

Sally

SALLY LIVINGSTON

Published by Author Academy Elite
PO Box 43, Powell, OH 43035
www.AuthorAcademyElite.com

Identifiers:
LCCN: 2019909776
ISBN: 978-1-64085-782-7 (paperback)
ISBN: 978-1-64085-783-4 (hardback)
ISBN: 978-1-64085-784-1 (ebook)

Available in paperback, hardback, e-book, and audiobook

Dedication

I want to thank every person who willingly sat in a chair in front of me and bravely shared their story. I have been blessed beyond measure through the courage you possessed to open up to the process of healing. Thank you for inviting me in to walk those complicated steps with you.

It is my prayer that the words on these pages and the message of His hope find their way into the hands and hearts of those who are tired or discouraged, or feel trapped by their *it*.

Contents

SECTION II: THE SOLUTION OFFERED – FOUR STEPS

SECTION THREE: LIVING LIFE UNSTUCK

Acknowledgments

I cannot thank my parents enough for teaching me to trust God, to work hard and never give up. I cherish them and our friendship.

I thank my husband, Scott for his love and support in this process and all of our life together. Thank you to my three remarkable adult children whom we birthed, but God raised. To Leah (and son-in-law Taylor), Andrew and Sarah, you have all given me inspiration and focus and most of all, love and support.

Thank you to my writing cheerleaders, Georgia, Rosy, Robert, Debbie and Barbra. They never stopped encouraging me or believing this would become a reality – even when I was not so sure.

I am grateful to the team at AAE: Kary, Niccie, Brenda, Abigail, Emily, and Nanette for the inspiration and encouragement to dream this dream, and for the tools to make it a reality.

To my most wonderful editor, Felicity, I cannot give enough praise. I so appreciate the positivity and dedication she brought to sharpening the words on the pages and the graceful partnership that made this book better than it was when she received it.

Above all, I thank God for His unfailing love. He is my Source, and I cannot do anything without Him, but all things through Him.

Introduction

Have you ever played the "when I was your age" game? You may have played without realizing it at the time. It is likely that someone said to you, "when I was young, I had to walk two miles in the snow to school." Have you heard, "when I was your age, we didn't have cell phones or the internet. We had to look things up in books at the library." Did you hear the commentary about friends and communication? "We had to meet people in-person to call them friends, and we had to wait to call someone when the phone wasn't in use by someone else in the house. If we heard a busy signal, we had to wait to speak to them." Likely, the person who dragged you unknowingly into this "game" was a bit older than you. Maybe the story was embellished to make them seem more oppressed, to engender feelings of admiration, sympathy for the hardship, or a bit of humility for you. The idea behind all of the statements is resilience. In essence, they made it through despite the challenges. If they can do it, so can you! (Typically, the older generation thinks the younger one has it easier, but that is another story!) The ultimate purpose of "when I was your age" stories is to inspire or challenge the listeners to look at their circumstances, check their perspective, and view the obstacles in a new light. These stories are meant to encourage "can do" thinking and turn difficulties into opportunities.

Not long ago, we lived in an age of self-determination marked by "because I can" thinking. There was real optimism about dreams and the ability to accomplish them. We heralded stories of people in extreme circumstances rising and overcoming. Now we are living in a time of resignation. We chastise accomplishment and vilify success in favor of victimhood. Instead of "because I can" thinking, we receive excuses why we shouldn't be held responsible for not even trying. Today, the rationale is to excuse a lack of effort. When there is snow and a two-mile walk, we cannot and should not do anything. Stay safe and dry where you are. Save your energy. Enjoy some hot chocolate and marshmallows and don't stress about it! We focus more on the existence of the problem and how it started, rather than how to solve or move past it. We get fixated on what has happened to us and how we are fated to a life dictated by our experiences. However, our experiences correctly viewed could be an opportunity for lasting change and transformation.

We all have experiences or relationships that can act as barriers to successful living when we face difficult situations that act as a hindrance. It is now normal to find a reason why we cannot do better or reach higher, rather than look at what we can do to remove those barriers. In a strange way, we are in competition with one another regarding our stress levels, painful experiences, and past difficulties to validate our condition of being stuck. It seems we celebrate and identify with our problems, dare I say —even nurture them. We send the message, "You can't do that, and don't feel bad, don't even try." It's almost as if we coddle our dysfunction, accept it as our lot, and thereby allow it to determine who we are and what we can or cannot do.

Before you go any further in this book, please hear me loud and clear on this point:

There are undoubtedly traumatic and devastating events in life, which cause genuine, long-lasting suffering. There is absolute evil in our world, which may present itself with a tremendous, lifetime impact from childhood and beyond in unimaginable ways. However, this current cultural emphasis on claiming and living in a state of victimhood does nothing to help and encourages a resignation to be identified by, and stuck in the trauma. Victory over the issues and pains of our past or present comes when we take the necessary steps to move forward. In other words, ultimately, we have to move toward the problems in our way to get to the other side of them. Transformation *is* possible, but first, we have to "*Get Over It!*"

SECTION ONE

The Problem Defined – What's Your IT?

ONE

We Get Stuck

The Broken-Record Syndrome

"Oh, help!" said Pooh. "I'd better go back."
"Oh, bother!" said Pooh. "I shall have to go on."
"I can't do either!" said Pooh. "Oh, help and bother!"
                                        — Milne, A. A.

"Growth is painful. Change is painful. But, nothing is as pain-
ful as staying stuck where you do not belong."
                                        — N. R. Narayana Murthy

"**W**hat brings you here today?" It is the question I often ask within the first few minutes of meeting someone in my office. Sometimes I ask the corollary question, "What do you want to get out of our time together?" My questions are meant to help crystallize the goal for the session and set a path for the counseling relationship. The goal is to create a destination point and a course for how to arrive there. In other words, the two questions could be: "Where have you been? Where are you?" and "Where are you going? Where do you want to end up?" Ultimately, "What is standing in the way of you moving toward that desired destination?"

When someone arrives at the point of seeing a therapist or confiding in someone, they realize something is not right in their life, and something is in the way of what they want and where they hoped to be. They talk with a therapist, a friend, or a pastor because they don't know how to change their situation. In other words, they feel stuck. For many, however, they don't realize this is the case, and they exist in this cycle of frustration, pain, and discouragement, thinking that it is just "life."

The first step to reaching goals or working to find solutions of any kind is to define the problem. Perhaps the most crucial step is to confirm there is a problem at all. What is the problem and to whom does it belong? In my 25 plus years as a psychotherapist, I encountered countless clients discouraged by a repetitive, impossible situation. They remain trapped, stuck like a broken record in the anger, shame, and resentment. They do not know how to move on. They enter into what I call the "stuck cycle." They don't want to feel pain, so they try to protect their feelings in the same way armor protects a body. The protection becomes like a bulletproof vest, not allowing anything to come through —including insight or help. They might know there is a problem, but defining it is often the first difficult task. There is a blockade in front of them they do not understand or know how to navigate. They utter something like, "I know I have to get over it," while hanging their head, releasing a heavy sigh, and lowering their eyes. They express a sense of personal shame and defeat. The problem is they genuinely don't know where to begin. In many cases, they have been coping with the issue for so long and have so closely identified with it; they may not even realize it is the source of the blockade because it has become "who they are."

Simply stated, we all get stuck sometimes, and we don't always know how to move on. When we feel incapable, we struggle with things we cannot understand and are unable to get past. While we all get stuck from time-to-time, the reasons we can't get past certain things vary widely. The experiences, however, are remarkably similar and very common.

> **Simply stated, we all get stuck sometimes, and we don't always know how to move on.**

God created us for connection. We are born longing for an intimate relationship with Him first and foremost because He wired us to desire love and a sense of belonging. We learn about relationships with others at this earliest stage because this desire translates to those closest to us. For many, this is where the stuck feeling starts. As much as I would like to say this is avoidable, it would require the impossible: perfect parenting and an ideal childhood. When this vital first experience of connection is strained, broken, breached, or violated, we may feel shame and unworthiness. Often, disconnection leaves us feeling unloved and worse, unlovable.

We feel threatened in our sense of connection if we feel like the "different one" in the family or when something is overtly abusive. The Enemy delights in every one of these opportunities to disconnect us, as it is his sole purpose to steal, kill, and destroy our ability to be in connection. ("A thief is only there to steal and kill and destroy. I came so they can have real and eternal life, more and better life than they ever dreamed of." John 10:10 MSG) If left unresolved, this disconnection continues to manifest itself in all the relationships that follow. It becomes the established narrative, ultimately leaving us stuck and unable to live in the freedom Christ gave us through His sacrifice on the Cross.

What are the "it" or "its" in your life that you are not able to get past? What is the issue, relationship, or set of behaviors that continually loop in your life? What's your story?

What hurt you? What hit you hard? What has you stuck? The "what's" will be addressed more fully in the subsequent chapters. For now, let's focus on the fact that some times and in some ways, we all get stuck.

When I was growing up, I used to love to listen to vinyl disc records in my room. I sang at the top of my lungs! (I know I'm dating myself with this story. Now they are sold in some stores marketed as "vintage," a kind word for old-fashioned.). It was not unusual for the record to "skip" or repeat. I stopped singing to attend to the record player to keep the music playing. When there is foreign matter in the groove of the record, it disrupts the normal progression of the song. The needle needs the gunk cleaned out of the slot, or the arm has to be lifted and replaced. This story is a metaphor for how we get stuck with our "it." I know records are not common anymore, so this visual may not translate well for some. Imagine attempting to live stream or download video content but continuously receiving an irritating rotating wheel icon. The wheel indicates the video is buffering, another word for "hold on—this content is stuck, and so are you." It would be easy if getting "unstuck" in our lives simply meant lifting the record player arm or waiting for the video content to load.

When we are stuck, why do we stay stuck? Here are a few possible explanations:

- We don't know what's on the other side. We are afraid of the unknown.

- We don't know if it's worth all the work it'll require to arrive on the other side. We have no roadmap for getting there.

- We get used to coping with it, living in the "functional happiness." Scientists discovered negative emotions have an addictive quality, which can trigger the reward centers in the brain. Worry, shame, guilt, and pride are triggers in the reward center of the brain. As a result, harmful emotions can feel good on some level.

- We made efforts and failed, and we are afraid to try again.

- We don't think it's a big deal and we hope it will just work itself out.

- Family and friends say, "find a way to live with it."

- We may feel God is punishing us for some behavior.

- The familiar is comfortable. We are creatures of habit and strive for equilibrium, even if it means remaining captive to what we know. Fear of the unknown outweighs the desire for freedom.

- We deny the presence or the impact of the event that has us stuck.

- We internalize it, and it becomes our label.

- We detach from it and live in a disjointed double world.

- We avoid it altogether.

Trauma is defined as a deeply disturbing or distressing experience. Merriam-Webster's definition ranges from:

1b: a disordered psychic or behavioral state resulting from severe mental or emotional stress or physical injury
to
1c : an emotional upset

Based on these definitions, we have all experienced some level of trauma. It's safe to say we have all been emotionally upset. Traumatic experiences can range from things we consider to be normal life, to things like war and terrorism. Whether the upset stems from reasonable, expected life issues, or it is from something unimaginable and unfathomable, the outcome can be trauma.

"Whatever the source, trauma leaves its imprint on the brain. For example, research studies consistently show that post-traumatic stress disorder (PTSD) is linked to greater activity in brain areas that process fear and less activation in parts of the prefrontal cortex. When trauma occurs, people enter into a fight, flight, or freeze state, which can result in the prefrontal cortex shutting down. The brain becomes somewhat disorganized and overwhelmed because of the trauma, while the body goes into a survival mode and shuts down the higher reasoning and language structures of the brain. The result of the metabolic shutdown is a profound imprinted stress response." (Psychology Today article by Seth Gillihan in Sept 2016)

There are some truths the brain refuses to process. The brain acts as a protective shield —it "shuts down" in part to keep us safe from the trauma and from having to deal overtly with the overwhelming fear, pain, and panic at the moment.

There are some truths the brain refuses to process.

It creates walls we can stay behind while the enemy fire is coming our way. The body and mind experience a numbing, self-protective response to overwhelming events. The walls protect us in those moments, but they can also prevent help from arriving. To heal, the power is in acknowledging what is hidden. It allows us to see clearly and use the clarity to take action. Ultimately, it helps us to clean up the faulty storyline we are living that tells us we are stuck and have to stay there.

Bessel Van Der Kolk, a leading psychiatrist in the trauma field, addressed this issue. He spoke about the importance of acting in the face of trauma. He said, "taking action is the core issue…It's in action that people take back their power and create healing, and words cannot substitute for action."

Why is it so hard to take action, to move on from our "it?" Sometimes we are confused about what "it" is and sometimes, we have lived with it so long we cannot even recognize "it." We tend to normalize the trauma and pain. We let it become our understanding of the world. It becomes the foundation on which we stand and operate. We make up stories based on this false narrative. It's what we know and who we think we are. It is as if we have a team jersey we received in childhood, it is ill-fitting, but if we keep it on long enough, it is comfortable and we believe it is our identity. As long as we wear it, we are fixed underneath it, unable or unwilling to look at the wounds it creates. The unrealized and unhealed wounds keep us mentally and emotionally imprisoned. To heal, we must face our "it" by name and seek to build a new foundation.

A compelling reason we stay stuck is our desire to know *why* we are stuck in the first place. We prolong or postpone any productive action waiting for a reason, *why*. We can't help but ask ourselves, those around us, and God, "why" or "why me" and beg Him for the answer to give us meaning, understanding or relief. The question is natural, but it is like quicksand. We flail about in despair and sink deeper into the sand and muck, hoping for the right answer to pull us out. We believe if we understand why, then we will feel better and be able to move on. This is a mistaken notion because the explanation does not remove the pain, resolve the issue, or relieve us. Even if we do understand why the answer may not be to our satisfaction. The better question is: "what next?" This question has forward movement and promises a strategy for the next steps. "What next?" sets us up to get over it!

Remember, there is an Enemy we face, and he wants us stuck. It is a spiritual battle. He wants us to question God and never quite understand how we can move past these things. He is the enemy of freedom and truth. He uses fear, anxiety, worries, and doubts to keep us stuck. It is important to note that "stuck" is not a condition, nor is it a disease. It is a state of the heart and the mind. What we do in this state can be destructive and habitual. When we understand it is a state of mind and heart, we have access to the power to get over it! We read about this in 2 Timothy.

"For God has not given us the spirit of fear; but of power, and of love, and of a sound mind." 2 Timothy 1:7 (KJV)

Fear is a state of mind and heart we all experience. In fear, we are unable to think clearly, to dream, to love well, or to take action. In summary, we are stuck sometimes—frozen in our pain, our past, and our situation. God's Word tells us we don't have to stay that way. He says we can be free. John 8:36 (NIV) says,"So if the Son sets you free, you will be free indeed."

Fear is a state of mind and heart we all experience. In fear, we are unable to think clearly, to dream, to love well, or to take action

In other words, we can let it go! Now, I realize these words probably conjure up images of the popular Disney movie Frozen about sisters Elsa and Anna and a singing snowman. I apologize if you've finally moved past this song and now I restarted the player. However, it's a great reminder when we are stuck, there is a response we have within our power, an action we can take to move to the other side.

Before we dive into the steps to take to get over your "it," let's take a little detour to talk about the origin of the stuck cycle.

TWO

Where "The Stuck" Gets Started

No Place like Home

"Anybody who has survived his childhood has enough information about life to last him the rest of his days."
— Flannery O'Connor, <u>Mysteries and Manners:</u>
<u>Occasional Prose</u>

"One of the pitfalls of childhood is that one doesn't have to understand something to feel it. By the time the mind is able to comprehend what has happened, the wounds of the heart are already too deep."
— Carlos Ruiz Zafón, <u>The Shadow of the Wind</u>

"Children are like wet cement, whatever falls on them makes an impression."
— Haim Ginott

"There's no place like home." It's a memorable line from a famous movie, *The Wizard of Oz*. It takes us to Oz, Dorothy, Toto, and the yellow brick road. You may notice I purposely left out the angry green person I will not name. Okay, full disclosure here—that character represents a traumatic memory for me. There was a woman in the church I grew up in who was the spitting image of that green person in the movie. No, she wasn't green, and she didn't have a black pointed hat or any flying monkeys hanging around her —but as a child walking through the Wednesday night dinner line, I was sure it was her. I was also deeply impacted by the shark in the movie Jaws, but I digress. "There's no place like home" resonates with us. We hear the line and feel something. We look back with some longing or nostalgia, and we reminisce.

Home is not just a place. Home is a collection of people, memories, sights, sounds, tastes, and experiences. The word home conjures up something different for each of us. Think of the word home. Now, close your eyes. What do you see, hear, feel, and smell? Home represents family, for good or for bad, and the experiences that shaped you and gave you the earliest ideas about who you are. It represents what you value and what you believe. It shaped your identity.

Our earlier experiences are when the stuck began. What the word home means to you has so much to do with who you are today. It influences how you get along in the world and what you recreate in your relational life. Remember, God designed us for relationships with a desire to belong and to be connected. This earliest connection point is where you came from, what you learned, and what you took from the experience. It is the basis from which you now view home, family, and all relationships for better or for worse.

As a Marriage and Family Therapist, when people ask who I see, I used to say I mostly help couples, but I also see anyone having relational issues. After so many years in the field, I realize when you get right down to it, all therapy is family therapy. It's the 42-year-old married man who cannot get past his childhood shame to receive love from his wife, while his wife learned to make everything "nice" for everyone else while she lived in silent pain and emptiness. It's the 45-year-old woman who learned not to trust anyone, and therefore she's never been in a relationship. It's those abusing substances, the person having an affair, or even the 14-year-old with extreme anxiety. It's all family therapy. Let's start there.

The family serves as a crucial part of God's plans on earth. The family is how God communicates, preserves, and further expands His holy influence. The home is the place where His truths are taught and followed. It has never been more challenging to have a healthy family life than it is today. There are numerous distractions, and the family is under assault today like never before. The ability to parent children is confused and challenged by schools, government, and culture. The Enemy comes to kill, steal, and destroy. His number one target is the family unit, particularly the head of the family; the marriage relationship. The goal is to destroy society, which starts by destroying the family. We see the effects of destruction and tragedies in families like never before. In the news, we hear of children as young as 11 wanting to commit suicide because they feel hopeless. Kids shoot up their schools, and parents hold their children hostage for years on end. How can you emerge from your family or start one with so much destruction?

We all came from a family. Regardless of the structure, we had caretakers responsible for our earliest stage of care. Our earliest teachings shaped who we are. From their first glance into our eyes, our parents told us who we are and set the tone for our lives. From that moment to every exchange that followed, the earliest experiences impacted what we believe, how we behave, and the outcomes we will have as a result.

We seek to answer the question, "Who am I?" in the context of this first relational experience.

You should not underestimate the impacts of your earliest family experiences. In case you aren't convinced, walk through this list of questions related to the family you grew up with.

Make a mental check of all statements that apply:

- Did you experience recurrent emotional abuse as a kid?

- Physical?

- Sexual?

- Did you experience physical neglect?

- Emotional neglect?

- Did anyone in your childhood home have substance abuse issues?

- Did anyone struggle with mental illness?

- Did anyone participate in criminal behavior and/or go to jail?

- Was your mother ever treated violently?

- Did you experience divorce or parental separation?

How many checks do you have? Clinicians refer to this as your ACE score. ACE stands for "adverse childhood experiences," and countless studies confirm it has a significant influence on your lifetime health. The life expectancy of individuals with ACE scores of six or more is twenty years less than it is for people with no ACEs. A person with four or more ACEs is twice as likely to develop heart disease and cancer, and five times as likely to suffer depression. One out of eight children undergo enough trauma to face lasting damage and are at risk for physical, mental, social, and health difficulties.

You might assume that someone who had a hard childhood might not make the most self-preserving choices or have access to quality healthcare. What's not so intuitive is the presence of these kinds of experiences at a young age changes the body's physiology. It floods the still-developing system with cortisol, changing the way the body deals with stress forever. It throws the hormonal processes out of whack and can create thyroid disorders. It impairs the regulatory mechanism of the immune system and even turns specific genes on and off.

The young body *really* remembers. While adults who experience something traumatic are often capable of re-wiring their stress response over time, the severity and stubbornness of the effects of trauma on children are more potent. Pediatrician, Dr. Nadine Burke Harris explains in her book, *The Deepest Well: Healing the Long-Term Effects of Childhood Adversity*, "The difference between adaptive and maladaptive reactions is all about the *when*. When little children are constantly exposed to what is often referred to as "toxic stress," it can cause a wide range of problems immediately—obesity, growth failure, ADHD etc.—and an even wider range over time. Their systems are so in flux, so vulnerable." The existence of chaos, threat, inconsistency, and uncertainty in a home wire the young brain to be more susceptible to mental health problems, and severely impacts one's level of functioning. In other words, children are highly sensitive to developmental trauma. When trauma happens in childhood, the child inevitably believes they are partially responsible. Because children are egocentric, they always ask, "What's wrong with me?" If the question is ignored and not corrected, the child wears the, "I'm wrong" jersey into adulthood, not knowing any differently.

This list may seem real for some and extreme for others. You may be exempt from particular outcomes. Be certain, however, your earliest family life impacted you. As the expression goes, no one escapes family unscathed.

The family is a system. Visualize a community pool. Now I know that can be an unpleasant thought. The community pool is shared by all those swimming in it. For the family, we can use a more helpful image, perhaps a backyard pool. All the family members swim in it. What is in the pool affects all those in it. In other words, a family acts as a system. What one person does has an impact on everyone else. The waves made at one end of the family pool make their way down to the other end. Children, in particular, are like sponges—they soak up everything. They are not able to discern what to take in or not, and everything is absorbed.

You've probably heard, "Fruit never falls far from the tree that bears it." In other words, we repeat what we see. We marry someone like our mother or our father. We repeat patterns and fall into cycles based on what we know.

If you aren't convinced or need an example, think about these:

- Are you good or bad with conflict? Where did you learn that?

- Is it easy for you to talk about sex, if so or if not, why?

- What is your view of marriage – is it based in some part on your parents' example?

- What do you eat or not eat just because you did or didn't as a child?

In my family, I didn't have a classic peanut butter and jelly sandwich. Yes, I had peanut butter. Yes, I had jelly. As a result, what do you think I gave to or withheld from my children? They didn't get the combination either. It seems like a silly thing, but the power of the pattern prevailed!

Family patterns and family history, including the behaviors and beliefs, repeat themselves most in our relational life. If you are unclear about who you are and where you came from, you'll revisit those habits and patterns in all of the relationships that follow. Whether intentionally or not, you will teach them to your children.

If you are unclear about who you are and where you came from, you'll revisit those habits and patterns in all of the relationships that follow. Whether intentionally or not, you will teach them to your children.

We try to resolve these unspoken childhood issues by acting them out in other relationships, especially in a marriage. If you are married, think about the things you do, and their relation to the roots which stem from your childhood home. Why do you behave and feel the way you do? Why do you buy the brands you buy, clean your house in the order you do, expect the behaviors from your spouse that you do?

We see a picture of the very first human relationship, the marriage and ultimately a family in the very first book of the Bible. In Genesis one, we read about God's creation of the earth and a place He prepared for the first couple. It is described as a garden called Eden. If you aren't familiar with it or it's been a while, go back and read the description of it. It sounds pretty amazing.

Imagine Eden. In our limited view of God's awesomeness, we can hardly do that. Let's start with something we might be able to understand or visualize. You've seen the commercials and gazed longingly at the beautiful scenery. There were beautiful couples, deeply in love, living in villas suspended over crystal-clear water with someone tending to their every need. Imagine Eden was the very first all-inclusive resort, but in the way only God would do it: lush and beautiful, full of anything you could want or need, beyond anything you can imagine and with no concern about money because everything was free. It is not a once in a lifetime vacation but forever. Adam and Eve, the first couple, were meant to live in Eden forever but something changed all of that.

God prepared a place, a home, a family for Adam and Eve. The Garden of Eden was the first home, one full of order, beauty, peace, harmony, love, and calm. Adam and Eve had a house built by God. It was beautiful, free from pain, guilt, worry, shame, work, or any distraction. They had the ultimate beauty of a direct and intimate connection with Him.

In Psalm 127 (NIV) we read about the building of a house.

> [1] Unless the Lord builds the house, the builders labor in vain.
> Unless the Lord watches over the city, the guards stand watch in vain.
> [2] In vain you rise early and stay up late,
> toiling for food to eat—for he grants sleep to those he loves.

In this passage, the word "house" may refer to an ordinary dwelling. It may refer to the temple as a place of worship, or it may be referring to a family. The statement is designed to indicate a universal dependence on God in the things we try to do as humans. The success of all our undertakings depends entirely upon God's blessing. It is in vain to attempt to build houses and cities, or to try to uphold families unless He prospers the design. The word vain is used here three times to emphasize the point that without God, our attempts are useless.

From this point on, we will use "house" to represent "home and family." God had a plan for family, and His plan was perfect. His was the designer and builder, and we were to follow and rely on Him. Let's look at the verse again from the Message version this time. I am especially interested in the first line:

Psalm 127 The Message (MSG)
127 ¹⁻² If God doesn't build the house,
the builders only build shacks.
If God doesn't guard the city,
the night watchman might as well nap.
It's useless to rise early and go to bed late,
and work your worried fingers to the bone.
Don't you know he enjoys
giving rest to those he loves?

God built them a house, but man's disobedience said, "I can do it myself! I can figure this out on my own." The self-reliant attitude exchanged God's plans for a house into a shack. Adam and Eve disobeyed God. They exchanged dependence on Him for independence, and the first family relationships suffered as a result. Immediately they began to experience chaos, fear, shame, guilt, pain, struggle, anger, rage, discord (and murder by chapter four). The repercussions of their choices quickly set in.

Can you imagine Eden with all its beauty and complete peace one minute, to expulsion the next minute, locked out for life? Imagine the presence of dense, pillowy earth, living in harmony with creatures, to a sudden transition to rocky ground, thorns and thistles, and animals who see you as prey. Now life would include strenuous work, strife, pain, suffering, and the assurance of death. If there was a marital argument, I imagine it happened the moment they stepped out of Eden. No doubt it was a doozy, probably loaded with accusations, finger-pointing, and blame. It may have sounded something like:

"Why did you give me that fruit…"
"This is all your fault."

"How could you blame me when God asked you about it?"

"Where were you anyway? You should have taken care of that snake."

Further in the story, we see that the first parenting effort didn't win any trophies. Son number one murdered son number two in a fit of rage, envy, and jealousy. The strife in the parental relationship was on display for the kids to see and experience. The brothers recreated it between one another. While we hope to avoid modeling dysfunction, it happens because we imitate what we know.

Let's get back to the shack. No one hunts for a shack, and no one builds one or throws shack-warming parties. No one has doormats or framed prints reading, "Shack, Sweet Shack." There are no popular shows titled "Shack Hunters" or magazines called "Shack Beautiful."

We may not desire a shack, but in many ways, we live with Shack Mentality. We depend on ourselves, we do it on our own and therefore settle for the shack instead of the beautiful design the Builder intended. Shacks have fragile, wobbly, and unstable foundations. When we stand on broken foundational bricks, we feel equally fragile, wobbly and unstable (see chapter 11 for more about these bricks).

*Disclaimer: This is not about blaming parents, or suggesting everyone has negative experiences at home. Our commonality lies within the moment the "it," and therefore, the brokenness entered our lives. We forfeited the Builder's perfect design. It's not that terrible parents created the "it" and in fact, it may not be what they did or didn't do. It may be more about your experience in the home with them. It may be a personality clash or perception of "should do" or "shouldn't do" behavior. Remember, your parents came from a broken model, too. The world was broken and brokenness causes pain. In short, we all have pain. What we do with the pain is key. Pain buried alive doesn't die—it grows until it breaks through the ground and likely, it replicates.

If you want to know the end of the story, look at the beginning. The only way to affect the ending of your story is to know where it began. It's

Pain buried alive doesn't die—it grows until it breaks through the ground and likely, it replicates.

essential to look at where you came from and your family. It will give you the information you will need to move past it and the knowledge to determine what to do in your future home and future family. Here's the hypothetical question. Was your family broken? The answer is a resounding yes for everyone because none of us come to adulthood without some level of brokenness, pain, or trauma. If we don't know or cannot acknowledge this reality, we turn a blind eye to the brokenness and perform the same behavior. We can only build from the tools our families handed down to us. If ours are not working and we feel stuck, it's time to take a look and replace them.

What can you do about all of this? How do you get those new tools? Take the first step: acknowledge where you came from, look for the source of trouble in your relationships. Look at the bumpy spots, where you get stuck and where the patterns appear. There is a theme.

When the car doesn't start, we usually assume there is a problem with the car battery. When the battery dies, the natural answer is to go down to the nearest auto mechanic and have it either charged if it still has life, or removed and replaced. It would be ridiculous to assume we have to push the car around. However, in life, often we "push the car" instead of replacing or charging the battery. We choose something so incredibly difficult, if not impossible, rather than going to the source of the problem. Instead of understanding the battery is bad, we expend all of our energy doing what will not work to keep moving. We focus on the wrong things when we don't understand the source of the problem. We get stuck when we don't look at the right things. The "shack mentality" is when we first get stuck. I invite you to look under the hood of your "family car." This invitation is not meant to blame, or bring up old pain or shame, but to offer you a chance to do something new for yourself and those in relationship with you—a chance to "change the battery."

We focus on the wrong things when we don't understand the source of the problem. We get stuck when we don't look at the right things.

To summarize, at the fall, the world was broken, and the family unit was forever changed. We are left to grapple with the question, who am I? We search for identity because the house the Lord built and His perfect plans for our stable home life were exchanged for a shack. We all were affected by our beginning, but how we feel about it will inevitably be impacted by what we first learned about feelings. How do you "feel" about your feelings? Let's look at that together.

THREE

The Trouble With Feelings

Feelings...nothing more than feelings

"Many falsely suppose that the feelings, which God has implanted in us as natural, proceed only from a defect. Accordingly the perfecting of believers does not depend on their casting off all feelings, but on their yielding to them and controlling them, only for proper reason."

— John Calvin

"The best and most beautiful things in this world cannot be seen or even heard, but must be felt with the heart."

— Helen Keller

"Though our feelings come and go, God's love for us does not."

— C. S. Lewis

I n the mid-1970s there was a popular song called "Feelings." It peaked at number six on the Hot 100 and was on the charts for 35 weeks, which broke the record at that time. It was a super sappy ballad about heartache and the loss of a relationship. It had a strangely catchy chorus that was hard to shake. The chorus repeated these lines:

Feelings…whoa whoa whoa (sung with a moaning quality similar to an animal howling at the moon)

Feelings….whoa whoa whoa (sung with even more gusto)

Take a listen, but be careful! You may not be able to get it out of your head! The song didn't have an abundance of lyrics and is probably on most karaoke song lists because the "whoa whoas" are catchy, easy to belt out, usually off-key, and in unison with everyone else in the room. Remarkably, it was sung by some pretty respectable singers through the years including Ella Fitzgerald and Julio Iglesias. The song has been used in movies and TV shows for comic effect, rather than musical value. The first line of the song, "Feelings, nothing more than feelings" implies ease, but it's a true statement. Feelings are feelings; plain and simple. It's easier to say this than to believe because feelings can be a touchy issue. For some, singing "Feelings" at karaoke night might be the closest to interacting with feelings they have ever come.

We have a complicated relationship with our feelings. This relationship is conditioned early in our lives as we spoke about in the last chapter. As infants and young children, feelings are a natural part of us, and the response is equally natural. We feel sad, hungry, lonely, mad, and we cry. We feel happy, and we smile or laugh. We aren't aware feelings can be wrong or negative. We don't think we need to change or suppress them until we hear, "Don't cry about that," or "You shouldn't feel that way," or "That's nothing to feel bad about," or "Others have it worse than you," or "That's selfish," or the big one: "It's a sin." While feelings are normal and God-given, unless educated on how to respond to them, we learn to betray them in deference to the response our earliest caretakers wanted or what we think they wanted. Unresolved feelings develop calluses. As a result, we become unaware of unresolved feelings.

Feelings are like fire. Fire is used to do good things: it provides warmth, fuel, cooks food, and refines. Forest fires can be **Unresolved feelings develop calluses. As a result, we become unaware of unresolved feelings.** healing or regenerative, or they can be extremely destructive. It is written: "fire is a good servant but a bad master." When under control, it is a useful tool, but out of control, it can destroy everything it touches.

There are generally two schools of thought when it comes to feelings—two camps, if you will. One camp says "feelings are nothing," and the other, "feelings are everything." The "feelings are everything" camp says, "If you feel it, do it. Flow with your feelings, let them guide you. Follow your feelings to know the truth." Feelings drive this camp, and they often wait to feel before they act. Feelings are an excuse for their behavior and a reason for their choices.

The "feelings are nothing" camp says, "What feelings? I don't have feelings. Feelings are bad, and they take over you if you let them, so don't feel." Ignore, deny, minimize, spiritualize, and subvert your feelings but whatever you do, don't let them out. A friend I used to work with is in the "feelings are nothing" camp. He used to make remarks like, "sure I have feelings and I can name all three of them, and if forced to, I know how to use two of them." The "feelings are nothing" camp may have members who joined reluctantly. Early on, they realized expressing their feelings brought them consequences they did not like, or could not bear. They may have decided it was better to deny all feelings and therefore avoid the pain of dealing with unpleasant consequences. They become like the little Dutch boy in the fictional story by Mary Elizabeth Mapes Dodge. Holland, being mainly below sea level, had a history of flooding in the Middle Ages, so they built a system of dikes to hold back the water. The story tells of a little boy who was walking by a dike and saw a leak. He put his finger in the hole, hoping to stop the water from coming through and destroying everything in its path. It was heroic to try to save the country from another flood, but as a result of his actions, he was stuck! Research shows that dikes don't usually leak, they would more likely weaken, and whole sections would give way at once. The imagery, though, is valuable to our discussion. Putting a finger in the dike to prevent the flow of water is like trying to deny or hold back feelings. For one thing, there would not be enough fingers available to stop the feelings from coming. Even so, trying to "plug the holes" would not prevent the flow—it would not make the water on the other side magically go away. This effort would only delay the inevitable redirection of the water and the weakening of the structure holding it back. In this case, it would weaken the person trying to hold it all back. When the structure gives way—and it always does—the water/the feelings come out with a vengeance and can create quite a mess.

As with all extreme positions, the truth lies somewhere in the middle. God gives us that middle lane between the two extremes, it is balanced and sequential.

In the Bible, we read that we are to "be angry and sin not."

Be ye angry, and sin not: let not the sun go down upon your wrath:

Ephesians 4:26 American Standard Version (ASV)

Go ahead and be angry. You do well to be angry—but don't use your anger as fuel for revenge. And don't stay angry. Don't go to bed angry. Don't give the Devil that kind of foothold in your life.

Ephesians 4:26-27 The Message (MSG)

There are two steps related to the emotion and expression of feelings found within these passages. Step one can be divided into two parts.

A: Accept that you have feelings and it is okay to do so.

B: Call it by name.

Let's use the emotion of anger found in the verse above, but it can be exchanged for any emotion in this process. Anger is one of the most easily accessible emotions and perhaps the one most easily misunderstood and misused. Unchecked anger is dangerous and can cause great harm; uncontrolled anger creates fear and destroys relationships. Anger does not have to be unchecked or uncontrolled if we understand it in the proper context. It is an indicator that something is wrong in the same way as the light that goes off in your car indicates the need for air in the tires or an oil change.

Somehow, we skip past the first words in this verse and focus on what follows. We don't hear the "do," but we understand the "don't." It can sound like, "Don't be angry." We translate it as anger is a sin, which is not true and not what the verse conveys. Many have the reflex thought: "If I am angry, I'm doing something wrong. I'm sinning, I'm bad." Be angry. Sin not. They are two separate statements describing two different responses. These are action verbs indicating choice and intent. The verse delineates the difference between the emotion of the feeling and its expression. The first statement says to "be angry." This means accepting it's okay and necessary to feel what we feel, to look at the light on the dashboard and see what it is calling us to attend to. It requires the awareness of the feeling. Feel it, own it, know it, and accept it. In fact, without this acceptance and knowledge, we are not able to take the second step. Without the acceptance of the first step, the second is more likely to be an automatic response with little to no control over it. It is likely to be what you have seen or were taught related to feelings when growing up. It comes out sideways and is not usually honest. If you don't allow yourself to feel (what you are already feeling), you will not be able to respond to the feeling in a healthy and honest way. The suppression of our emotions also suppresses our ability to respond in a way that we want to. It is like submerging a beach ball under the water which feels easy at first. But, after time, your arms cramp up, and the balance becomes impossible. When the ball inevitably comes up, it is with much more force than it would be if we hadn't been holding it under so long. The splash it creates is uncontrolled and far-reaching. Suppressed anger is like the beach ball under water. It comes up unexpectedly with force and a larger than proportional splash. The freedom to feel is so important—in exchange it allows us the freedom to choose our response.

> If you don't allow yourself to feel (what you are already feeling), you will not be able to respond to the feeling in a healthy and honest way.

Be aware of your feelings and then name them. This can be hard to do, but extremely important. Putting a name to your feelings can sound as sappy as the song we talked about previously. Maybe you'll roll your eyes and wonder what good it would do. I'm the first to say that sometimes it can sound like "psychobabble," and a throw-off comment with no application. Go ahead and roll your eyes, but hang with me—I promise you'll be glad you did. When you take this step, you will be able to make progress in *getting over*. The goal in naming the feelings is not just to feel them or give them unlimited power or to live as a slave to them, but to activate the planning center of the brain, which allows us to take action. Psychologist Dr. Henry Cloud says it this way, *"When you name a feeling it increases your brain's ability to deal with it."* If you have denied, ignored or suppressed your feelings, or if you carry others feelings instead of your own, then this is a very difficult step. It is difficult, but not impossible. It is learned behavior and the good news is it can be relearned in a healthy way. The question, "what do I feel?" goes a long way to beginning the process of feelings awareness. Feel what you feel, name it and then you can decide what to do with the feelings.

The freedom to feel is so important—in exchange it allows us the freedom to choose our response.

We "should" ourselves when it comes to feelings, meaning we "should" feel this and "shouldn't" feel that. When we listen to the "should," we stop the healthy sequence of dealing with our feelings, and instead, we end up stationary again. We try to quickly jump from what we are feeling directly into action without giving the heart any time to respond. The response in a "should" situation is not likely voluntary, but one from pressure or obligation. Should is similar to a demand, a lost opportunity to think and weigh options. Substitute the word "could" for "should" for a grace-giving and option-oriented action. When we know we don't *have* to, our choice is informed and free. With "could," we can own the choices and feel less stuck.

We see a precedent for allowing and acknowledging feelings in the book of Psalms, and most notably from the author of a good majority of its chapters, David. He and the other psalmists poured their heart out to God. There are honest and very raw emotions expressed in every chapter: deep disappointment, anger, confusion, sadness, loneliness, joy, excitement, and rejoicing. The honest emotions expressed in the Psalms help give us the freedom to be emotionally honest with ourselves and to present those emotions to God.

Maybe I can replace the *whoa whoa whoas* I've put in your head with the song, "Feelings." The message in Riley Clemmons' song, "Broken Prayers," is definitely more helpful and truthful regarding our feelings:

But You're not afraid of all the things I feel
So why am I afraid of being real?

You want my tears, every messy word
Every scar and every fear
'Cause You see the beauty
In my broken prayers!

After the feeling of emotion is handled honestly, we are able to move to step two, the expression of the emotion. We are able to decide what to do with the feelings: We will look more at this process in chapter eight, but for now it is important to note that after the emotion of feelings comes the opportunity for the healthy expression of them.

If you have ever repeated a cycle of trying but failing to move past something, or being unable to effectively deal with the emotions, (which I suggest most of us have), it may have been in that context that you first heard or said those three little words: get over it!

FOUR

Three Little Words

Mean or Magic?

"Getting over a painful experience is much like crossing monkey bars: you have to let go at some point in order to move forward."
— *C. S. Lewis*

"I tell you the past is a bucket of ashes, so live not in your yesterdays, not just for tomorrow, but in the here and now. Keep moving and forget the post mortems; and remember, no one can get the jump on the future."
— *Carl Sandburg*

"**G**et over it!" How do you feel when you read those words? Are you encouraged? Do you have the sensation of a pit in your stomach? Does it sound like sweet nothings whispered in your ear or an air horn blowing you away? We almost cannot read these words without feeling chastised, yelled at or spoken to in an angry tone. Close your eyes and imagine hearing these words. What comes to your mind? Who is saying it? What do you hear? It is common to picture pointed fingers, shouting, contorted faces, and fits of anger. These three little words are commonplace—we can imagine them, even if we have never actually heard them. We can easily say the phrase to someone or some group we do not know, especially on social media sites anonymously. However, it's not easy to say these words in person, because they sound harsh or mean.

There are similar expressions:

- "Move on."
- "Cry me a river."
- "It is what it is."
- "Don't cry over spilled milk."
- "Tough luck."
- "Who cares?"
- "Suck it up, buttercup."
- "Grow up."
- "Whatever."
- "Shut up."
- "Put on your big girl/big boy pants."

Wow, those are affirming words, aren't they? Don't they make you feel all warm and fuzzy?

The definition of "get over it" from the Urban Dictionary reads:

*"A **phrase** often said with sarcasm to someone without thinking of their feelings or reactions."*

I asked you earlier to imagine hearing this phrase and what it made you feel, but maybe you don't have to imagine it. Have you ever had the above words directed your way? How did it make you feel? Misunderstood? Judged? Accused? Dismissed? Alone? Were you more motivated to move from the problem to a resolution? Chances are, like most people, these words didn't motivate you. Instead, they created guilt, shame, embarrassment and a host of other negative emotions resulting in a desire to hide, which can lead to immobilization. Additionally, you are less likely to continue talking about your problem due to a lack of interest and unwillingness to listen.

Have you ever wanted to say the phrase to someone but you refrained? You didn't say it because you are a "nice person" with a heart, and it wouldn't be right. However, the phrase crosses the mind of every parent, boss, employee, friend, and therapist (yes, confessions of a therapist). Why is this the case? Initially, when presented with an complaint, concern, or issue, we are eager to listen and offer help. We spend time and energy offering solutions. However, when the issue is obsessively repeated, without an attempt to make a change, all future conversations feel repetitive, and the words may cross your mind. Ultimately, you may distance yourself altogether in an attempt to avoid future redundant conversations or hurting the person with the issue.

Our idea of hurting someone can be confused, even backwards. It is more hurtful to distance ourselves than it is to offer the truth. Maybe they *do* need to get over it, and we should say so. In our attempt to be "nice," we are not being honest and potentially causing more hurt to the person. We read in Proverbs 27:6 (ESV), "Faithful are the wounds of a friend...profuse are the kisses of an enemy". Though it is

> In our attempt to be "nice," we are not being honest and potentially causing more hurt to the person.

hard to do, speaking the truth is better than offering the pretense that may harm.

"Why can't you move on?" and "why don't you get over it?" This question may be genuine. The motivation, however, may be less about the answer to the question but rather a desired response. The intent is to encourage the person to stop having or talking about a problem. Stop thinking about it—ignore it; but be over it already. What a contradiction.

As we discussed earlier, the impulse to tell someone to "get over it" comes when we get to the point of exasperation and say this phrase in a way that means—don't talk to me about this anymore—I'm tired of hearing about it. We utter this phrase in a way that is less compassionate than we want it to be, and the message is not helpful and can be harmful. This is such a shame because it has the potential to be a powerful motivator if said this way: don't concern yourself with or stay in something that's already in the past; work to accept it and move on to more productive pursuits. Hebrews 10:24 (NIV) reads, "and let us consider how we may spur one another on toward love and good deeds." It would be more beneficial if we could honestly approach one another with this phrase, to encourage one another, to inspire growth or movement.

> **What if the words "get over it!" were not used as the last word—as the last gasp—but as the first to give life and encourage real change or growth?**

What if the words "get over it!" were not used as the last word—as the last gasp—but as the first to give life and encourage real change or growth?

How much better might it be to use this phrase proactively as a sense of encouragement? It communicates, "I believe in you" and "you can do this." It is about walking along with someone in the process rather than telling them or thinking they should be "over it" and then leaving him or her to deal with it alone.

There are, indeed, many issues people face that are extremely difficult to move past, such as: abuse, neglect, relational failure, pain, disappointment, disillusionment, anger guilt, and shame. Trauma is part of our world and will always be as we read in John 16:33 (NIV) "…in this godless world you will continue to experience difficulties…" Don't get me wrong. These issues are real and not to be diminished. The sentiment, though frustrated, has merit. In our culture, it is almost a badge of honor to have some issue to identify with and call on as the reason not to do something, or not to be where you want.

There are problems we *do* need to get over. We *can* deal with and move on from things. When used positively, the phrase is not suggesting, "don't deal with it" or "don't acknowledge the issues" and it is not meant to sweep bad behavior under the rug. It is not a "pull yourself up by the bootstraps" plan, nor is it a diminishment of genuine pain and suffering and the resulting impact. This approach is much more than a "positive thinking" notion. It speaks to the ability to understand your power over your mind, your choices, and your attitudes. Romans 12:2 tells us we have the responsibility to renew our minds. ("Do not conform to the pattern of this world, but be transformed by the renewing of your mind. Then you will be able to test and approve what God's will is—his good, pleasing and perfect will.") It is the most important thing to access the power of God and His Spirit within us. Scripture arms us for the battle of the mind if we access it and then choose to use its truth to help us get over it. It helps equip us to move to the new things God has for each of us.

In Isaiah 43:18-19 (NKJV), God spoke to His people through the prophet Isaiah. "Do not remember the former things, nor consider the things of old. Behold, I will do a new thing. Now it shall spring forth; shall you not know it? I will even make a road in the wilderness, and rivers in the desert."

Another version reads, "Remember not the former things, from them to take occasion, as some do, to undervalue the present things, as if the former days were better than these; no, you may, if you will, comparatively forget them, and yet know enough by the events of your own day to convince you that the Lord is God alone; for, behold, the Lord will do a new thing, no way inferior, both for the wonder and the worth of the mercy, to the things of old."

The Message Bible translation says it this way:

"This is what God says,
the God who builds a road right through the ocean,
who carves a path through pounding waves,
The God who summons horses and chariots and armies—
they lie down and then can't get up;
they're snuffed out like so many candles:
"Forget about what's happened;
don't keep going over old history.
Be alert, be present. I'm about to do something brand-new.
It's bursting out! Don't you see it?
There it is! I'm making a road through the desert,
rivers in the badlands.
Wild animals will say 'Thank you!'
—the coyotes and the buzzards—
Because I provided water in the desert,
rivers through the sun-baked earth,
Drinking water for the people I chose,
the people I made especially for myself,
a people custom-made to praise me."

This passage was a reminder to the Hebrew people in a time when they were captives in Egypt. Their situation was anything but good, and hope was all but lost. They were finally freed after many years and were being led out of bondage. Just when it must have seemed things were turning around, great danger of imminent death faced them again. They were tempted to look back at Egypt as if it were "not so bad," to even romanticize the horrible past based on fear of the present and hopelessness for the future. At just the right moment, with the full force of the Egyptian army heading toward them, God intervened and made the impossible possible. He built a road right through the ocean. This story is to encourage and remind God's people of His power and provision, despite the situation they face.

God is saying, as desperate as the situation seems and impossible for our minds to grasp any hope, He is doing a "new" thing. He is making a road through the desert, an impossible feat. The desert can have steep terrain and dunes as high as 820 feet. It is hard to walk in the sand on a beach, now imagine clearing dunes that high to create a road. God is in the business of making impossible things possible. We can trust it based on what He has done for His people in the past. He has it covered and will do it in a way that exceeds our expectations. He is also reminding us that we are His chosen people, and He is specific in meeting our needs. We can trust Him to help us let go of the past and move ahead or get over it.

As I considered writing this book, I heard the critics in my head. (The area I must get over.) The critics said, "It's not compassionate, or kind or professional to utter these three words, is it? How could you look at someone's deepest pain and hurt and tell them to get over it? How could you write a book encouraging people to simply get over their pain and past?" This is why we are stuck. The ones mired in the problem and the ones who wish to be part of the solution are helpless because the message sounds "mean." I would suggest that these three words may be the nicest "mean" thing you can say or hear.

These three words may be the nicest "mean" thing you can say or hear.

"Get over it!" can be a proactive statement that implies and encourages power. We cannot control all things that happen to us, and most certainly, there are horrific, and unfair, and wrong things. They should be called out as such. However, culture often encourages the label and creates a limited mindset. We live in a "stay stuck" culture. Victimhood is accepted as an excuse – almost an insignia we wear. We have normalized and subsidized being labeled by and fated by our "it." This is absolutely not the message of the Gospel. Jesus came to save us and set us free from all of the "its" we have experienced.

We have more power in Christ than we know. In Him we receive the power to give it over, and ultimately to get over it. This power is a mystery to many. We can more easily talk about the power of God than to understand or use it in our lives. We know He is powerful but we wait for Him to use His power to correct the problems in our lives. We don't always recognize that we possess His power within us in the form of His Spirit. When you receive Christ, you receive His Spirit to inform, encourage, and minister to you, but also to equip you for the battles ahead. God's work on the cross through Jesus opened the door for us to partake in the power.

We have the power to get over, but often we want to be done with it already and rush past the necessary process. This impatience or lack of knowledge leaves us stuck. You can't know where to go until you know where you came from and where you have been. You can't move past what you don't know is there or are unwilling to see. In case you do not see your "it" right now, here are some things you might want to consider "*getting over.*"

- *Getting over* your past. Let go of what you cannot undo; the hurts that you wear as truth that become your reason for the protective armor.

- *Getting over* your perceptions. We can have misperceptions based on faulty beliefs. Be sure you correctly see in the light of God's Word.

- *Getting over* your image. Let go of the image you hold that has been infected or warped and doesn't match God's image of you.

- *Getting over* your fears. God did not give that spirit to you and the Enemy uses it as His best tool to prevent you from moving forward.

- *Getting over* your faulty ideas. In Christ Jesus, "therefore, there is no more condemnation." In Him, we are not guilty or at fault and don't have to live under that illusion any longer.

As we move toward the how-tos of *getting over*, here is some necessary information as you gear up to get over:

- This is not a Band-aid or pain management—this is surgery. It requires going to the source and taking care of it once and for all. Tell yourself the truth, don't be afraid, trust the process.

- You will know you are over it when you no longer have to "tell the story." When it's not the thing you lead with or make excuses for, you are over it.

- You can't conquer what you refuse to confront. Be willing to name it and face it.

- Know the difference between identifying with the pain and the experience and letting it identify you. Let it be your experience, not your identity.

- You can actually drop it (the past). The past is over, and it can no longer hurt you. As one of the "philosophers" of our time so beautifully put it, "Shake It Off" (Taylor Swift).

- God is enough. He will be with you on the journey. We are to know Him and make Him known even in our difficult times.

Why is it essential we shift our ideas about this phrase? It could mean the difference between feeling stuck or being set free—between our identity tied up in the past or true freedom in the present carried into the future. Are you ready to take the next step? "Are you ready to jump the fences standing in your own way?"

FIVE

Jump The Fences

It's Your Choice

"Do not wait: the time will never be 'just right'. Start where you stand, and work whatever tools you may have at your command and better tools will be found as you go along."
— *Napoleon Hill*

"There are many ways of going forward, but only one way of standing still."
— *Franklin D. Roosevelt*

Get over it!

I saw a small laminated tray in a gift shop in Thomasville, Georgia, recently that caught my eye. As I was walking through the shop, I was stunned to find an item with these words, "Get Over It." I had been tangling with these exact words for the preceding months concerning this book you are currently reading. What was more interesting to me was the image on it, which gave me a new visual for the phrase, "Get Over It!" It was not the image I had envisioned of an angry person yelling at another person in exasperated tones. It was an entirely different concept and perspective. I decided to look into the image and learned it represented equestrian circles; it is related to a horse jumping over a hurdle and clearing it. It serves as a phrase of encouragement and empowerment for the rider. Showjumping has been an athletic sport in the Olympics since 1912. It requires a great deal of training and dedication. Success depends on knowledge of the hurdles—the height and distance between each one—and a strategy for how to manage and navigate your horse.

This leads us to those three little words: "Get Over It," and to two key questions.

1. What hurdles, fences, or barriers are in front of you? What is keeping you from living life to the fullest?

2. How do you want to handle the hurdles? Do you want to stay on this side of the barrier, or do you want to jump over, to get over?

The first question may have you stumped. For some of you, you know there is something there, but you can't quite put your finger on your "it." You may have been dealing with it for so long you are unable to see it. For others, the "it" is evident and plain to see. Maybe additional issues are stemming from the length of time it has been present.

Here are some of the "its" I have encountered in my life, my practice, and the lives of my friends and family. Maybe this list will help you identify or confirm yours.

- Abuse in childhood from parents (verbal, emotional, physical, sexual)
- Anxiety
- Insecurity in relationships (friendship or dating/married)
- Lack of confidence
- Self-esteem issues
- Self-worth/value issues
- Faulty beliefs causing conflict
- Fear
- Rejection

- Abandonment by parents
- Addiction
- Divorce
- Anger issues
- Death of a child (any time from pregnancy through adulthood)
- Death of a parent, friend, pet
- Sexual matters in marriage from past sexual trauma
- Trust issues
- Faith issues
- Relationship issues (friendship, dating)
- Fear/avoidance of conflict
- Physical injury/pain/illness
- Family enmeshment
- In-law pressures
- Boundary issues
- The pressure to make a big decision
- Job stress
- Marital conflict
- Perfectionism/Procrastination

The list goes on. It represents a wide range of issues ranging from minor irritants to devastating life traumas. Whatever your "it," if you're stuck, you can get over it if you first identify the hurdle.

The second question is not rhetorical. How do you want to handle the hurdle? It begs a conscious answer because a non-answer is also a course of action. It begins with acknowledging your position of power on how to respond, even if life happened *to* you. It requires an acceptance that this is the "horse" you are riding. You are in the saddle, on top of the horse with the reins in your hands. The two options are either immobilization because there is a hurdle, or mobilization, using your resources to move forward. Often, the hurdles we face in life are what we know and the filter through which we see the world. We make excuses not to jump the hurdle. Therefore, it is always in front of us. Over time, it appears insurmountable and impenetrable. As a therapist, I continuously encounter clients who realize their resilience once they lean on their skills instead of leaning on their former, "learned helplessness." It is almost as if they have never understood they have the option to jump, and the ability to move over to the other side. With encouragement and a few skills in their toolkit, they are better able to use their strength and to call on the power of God within them to take the reins and jump.

Again, there are two options. Do you take the reins and direct your horse when and where to jump the hurdles? Or, do you hold on for dear life while the horse runs around aimlessly? Life will continue to happen to you. A choice to view life from the tail of the horse, with mud and debris in your face, bruised and beaten up by the ground and the hooves, and possibly being the lucky recipient of the horse's natural bodily functions, is possible. (Quite a picture, isn't it?) Most of us would not choose that life willingly. The good news is we do have a choice! We can take responsibility for our lives, get on top of the horse, and take the reins which allows us to see what's ahead. We can direct our responses based on what comes in our path and where we want to go. The best news is God promises He will make our paths straight when we trust

Him wholeheartedly and lean on His truth and not on our own understanding.

> "Trust God from the bottom of your heart; don't try to figure out everything on your own. Listen for God's voice in everything you do, everywhere you go; he's the one who will keep you on track."
>
> Proverbs 3:5-6 (MSG)

The dictionary defines the phrase "get over" in the following ways:

Dictionary.com (British dictionary)

- to cross or surmount
- to recover from
- to overcome or master
- to appreciate fully

Merriam-Webster, American Standard Version

- To prevail against; overcome.
- To recover from: *finally got over the divorce.*
- To get across.

To "get over" involves a choice. All of these definitions are full of action verbs. To summarize, what can we prevail against, get across, overcome, surmount, appreciate fully, master, or overcome? What can we get over? Here are some possibilities:

- guilt

- shame

- fear

- insecurity

- disappointments

- relational failures

- faulty identity

- anxiety

- trauma

- pain

The phrase "get over it," if interpreted correctly, means, "Don't stay captive to your past. Don't stagnate in your present. Trust God for your future." The often-quoted line, "God loves me as I am but loves me too much to leave me that way" illustrates this concept. God loves you and me. He sees the things we are tied up in yet His love gives us the strength to live in freedom from those issues.

How is this going to work? What does get over it mean therapeutically?

I have watched people struggle with pain of every type and watched the progress arc in each of them. For many, the progress is extremely slow or intermittent at best. They remain in an endless cycle of trying but failing to get traction. This mentality eliminates any hope for change. Out of this journey, I have developed a systematic four-step-plan to help move people from feeling stuck to finding freedom from the "it." This idea came directly to me from God. I understand how it may sound, but I can say I had never received a clearer message. I was sitting in a new church in a brand-new city after moving 500 miles away from my home. The three words came to me first, then the idea for a four-step-plan. Although I was unsure what the outcome would be and I wrestled with the concept, I realized I was offering it more and more in real-time as a useful tool for working with clients who felt stationary, unable to make a decision, or something more serious. It seemed to help them map out goals and mark the progress strategically based on God's gospel message for all of us: We have a new life and identity in Christ because His presence in us brings freedom from our old life of sin and bondage.

From this point on in this book, we will use the term *getting over* as a motivational and encouraging phrase rather than in the context we covered in chapter four. I will refer to this as the *getting over* process. The next four chapters will cover the four-step process of moving past the "stuck" cycle. But first, a warning. It is easier said than done. I have attempted to make the steps in the next few chapters clear, concise, and easy to grasp. The concepts, though easy to understand, are much more challenging to put into practice. The process may take more than one cycle to work through depending on the history and entrenchment of the issue. With time and investment, however, these concepts will help you to Get O.V.E.R. your "it."

SECTION II

The Solution Offered – Four Steps

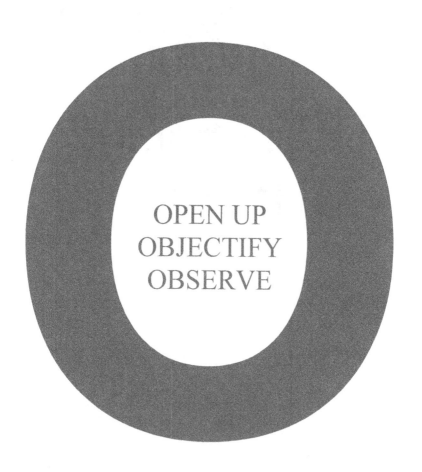

OPEN UP
OBJECTIFY
OBSERVE

SIX

Over: Objectify/Open Up/ Observe

What Happened?

"Objectivity requires taking subjectivity into account."
— *Lorraine Code*

"Dispassionate objectivity is itself a passion, for the real and for the truth."
— *Abraham Maslow*

For two consecutive summers, I spent a week in Quito, Ecuador, with my family on a mission trip. We spent most of the time working with the beautiful children of The Barrio. After we finished the week of work in the city, we had a day to celebrate with the team and explore. We drove toward the hacienda where we spent our last day and night, climbing in altitude as we went to the beautiful mountain range, the backdrop of our stay. We spent the day

51

on horseback, exploring the lower fields to take in one of the most spectacular views I have ever seen. The expanse of green grass and the rolling hills were surpassed in splendor only by the snow-peaked mountains. We stopped at the ultimate plateau and marveled at the sights before us. Later we ran our horses across the field in the exhilaration of the experience. It was one of "those moments" when you say, "God, you are so incredible, and I am so tiny." Another day we decided to climb Cotopaxi, a 19,000-foot mountain. We started with confidence, but the shifting soil, steep angle, thinning air, and temperature change made the journey difficult the higher we climbed. Despite the motivating scenic view, exhaustion inevitably set in, so we drove home that day, reveling in the notion that we had climbed a portion of this magnificent mountain. Though in reality, mountain isn't an accurate term to describe Cotopaxi. Cotopaxi is one of the highest active volcanoes in the world. It had been dormant for more than 70 years*, which is unusual for the pattern of eruptions in its history. Our beautiful and serene mountain range was volcanic and represented the possibility of extreme danger—what a contradiction.

The situations we face can appear as beautiful mountains when in reality, they are volcanoes. Volcanoes by nature are inherently dangerous, filled with lava and ash in their eruptive state. When dormant, they are deceptively peaceful. Many of our issues appear to us as erupting volcanoes disguised as beautiful, dormant mountains or beautiful, dormant mountains that present as erupting volcanoes. We need to think objectively to know the truth in our situations rather than assuming something is or must be because it always has been.

We can easily make mountains out of molehills and molehills out of mountains if we are not looking objectively.

We can easily make mountains out of molehills and molehills out of mountains if we are not looking objectively. (*as of the writing of this book, Cotopaxi began to erupt 6/15/15.)

The idioms, "seeing is believing," or "what you see is what you get," are not necessarily correct. We have natural biases and beliefs that cause us to see what we want to see or to avoid seeing what we do not want to see or cannot understand.

- *"The eye sees only what the mind is prepared to comprehend.*— "Henri Bergson (French philosopher)*

- *"To look backward for a while is to refresh the eye, to restore it, and to render it the more fit for its prime function of looking forward."*— Margaret Fairless Barber (1869-1901) author*

- *"It's not what you look at that matters, it's what you see."*— Henry David Thoreau*

- *"Stars and shadows ain't good to see by."*— <u>Mark Twain, The Adventures of Huckleberry Finn</u>*

- *"Seeing is never believing: we interpret what we see in the light of what we believe. Faith is confidence in God before you see God emerging, therefore the nature of faith is that it must be tried."*— Oswald Chambers*

How is it possible to move on from a "stuck" position to a place of freedom, over the "it?" The first step to *getting over* your "it" is to Objectify, Open up, and Observe. Give "it" a name; absorb it, notice the details, and be honest. Get clarity. Be objective, gain an accurate view of the situation. What do you see? What happened to you?

Have you heard the expression, "You can't conquer what you refuse to confront?" Many times, we are unable to deal with our "it" because we deny its existence or we don't understand what is happening. The first step is to own the truth about what the obstacle is, including what you are holding onto as a result: shame, guilt, the inability to trust—and then separate it from who you are.

When we live under the narrative of our childhood experiences, faulty foundations form from abuse, neglect, and other forms of trauma. Families often have an unspoken understanding, "We don't talk about those things" or "If you tell anyone, it will hurt you, or it will ruin our family." Secrets make us sick. A foundation based on secrets is insecure and fuels our "stuck" mentality. To take the first step to *getting over*, we must understand that it's okay to tell the truth even if we don't think we can handle it, or others won't like it.

Objectifying or externalizing a situation helps us to look at it from a distance or another perspective. How often are you able to advise others, but you cannot take your wise advice? It's always easier to see a situation clearly when it's labeled from a different perspective. What a gift we give to others when we help them see from an outside perspective. Wouldn't it be great to offer that gift to yourself?

Objectivity has some messages for you to consider:

- Your past doesn't define you; it prepares you for today and empowers you for tomorrow.

- You are not your experience; it happened to you but doesn't define you.

- You were victimized; you are not a victim.

- You are divorced; you are not your divorce.

- Your parents were not there for you; you are not rejectable.

- Your story isn't who you are; what you tell yourself about the story is what matters.

- You have failed; you are not a failure.

- You were devalued; you are not value-less.

- You have an addiction; you are not the addiction.

Objectification says, "no wonder you are having a hard time." It answers the question, "Why do I feel this way, act this way, have this problem?" Objectivity allows a "because," not as an excuse to stay there, but as an explanation for why we are there. Too often, we speak harshly about ourselves, but we give grace to others. Be the kind voice to yourself that you are to others.

Be the kind voice to yourself that you are to others.

It's been said:

- Your Test becomes your testimony.

- Your Mess becomes your message.

- Your Trial becomes your triumph.

- You can go from Stumbling block to stepping stone.

This type of progress only happens when you validate your feelings (more on that in the next chapter) about the situation, allowing yourself to objectify and observe it properly. It will enable you to open up to the one source of all truth, the one who gave His son for the ultimate validation of who you are and more importantly, who you are in Him.

"*Open up* before God, keep nothing back, He'll do whatever needs to be done. He'll validate your life in the clear light of day and stamp you with approval at high noon." - Psalm 37:5 (MSG)

"Open your mouth and taste, open your eyes and see—how good God is. Blessed are you who run to Him". - Psalm 34:8 The Message (MSG)

"Then you will know the truth, and the truth will set you free." - John 8:32 (NIV)

Open up to the truth of what you are facing—whether it is a difficult decision, relationship trouble or something more severe. It all matters because all of it plays a role in our lives. Set it on the table and **Observe** it. What happened to you or where you are stuck? Write it out as if you are taking notes about someone else's story. Get the who, what, why, where, and when of it on paper. Once it is in this physical form, you can see it as something that happened. Read it aloud. Respond to it like you would if it was someone else's story. Realize this is your account. This sounds obvious, but it is the first step for a reason—we get stuck because we don't know how or want to look at what happened. Therefore, we cannot deal with it productively. Be honest with yourself, look at it objectively, and then open up to safe and loving people about your "it." As a Christian, the worst and best thing has already occurred. We were sinners with no hope and separated by God as a result of our sin. When we accept the sacrifice Jesus made for us and receive Him as our bridge to God, we are declared not guilty. Romans 8:1 says: "We are no longer condemned when we are in Christ."

You cannot become who you are meant to be if you are looking back or wearing an old "jersey." Take it off and leave it off. God sees you in the now and the future—you are not in your past any longer. Identify your "it," but don't identify *with* or be identified *by* it. The first step allows you to understand why your feelings exist, and to see them accurately.

VENT
VALIDATE
VERIFY

SEVEN

oVer: Vent/Validate/Verify

What Was That like for You?

The sorrow which has no vent in tears may make other organs weep."

— *Francis J. Braceland*

"A man cannot be comfortable without his own approval."
— *Mark Twain*

While the first two steps in the OVER process are the hardest for many, the V step may be the toughest. Despite the fear and work, all steps are necessary to continue the process. The O and V steps (where the incident/accident happened and how it affected you) are required to get to the "other side" of the process to the E and R, represented in this book as the steps with forward momentum. Interestingly, E.R. is also the abbreviation for "emergency room," an area within a hospital to get help.

Step two in the *getting over* process is Vent, Validate and Verify,

VENT/Vocalize:

Step two addresses the feelings we have about what happened to us because we have to acknowledge our feelings before we can heal. There's an essential difference between dealing (coping) and healing. Coping is about getting by. It says, "I have to figure out how to handle this without getting too close to it." I see people coping in my practice when they recount something, and the emotions begin: tears well-up, the face flushes, and with all the strength they can muster, they swallow hard and push the emotion away. The client says with a sense of resignation, I know I just have to cope with this. This falls into the same category as *getting over it* because the interpretation is, "you are the problem, and you cannot move past it. If only you could do what you cannot or do not know how to do, you would be fine." Quite a messy way to think, right? Coping is the loop we can be stuck in forever, and dealing is the arrow pointing forward that shows us the way to *getting over* and helps us take the necessary steps. We choose to cope rather than deal when we don't want to face the emotions.

The word vent is defined this way:

noun

- 1. an opening that allows air, gas, or liquid to pass out of or into a confined space.

- 2. the expression or release of a strong emotion, energy, etc.: "children give **vent** to their anger in various ways"

verb

- 1. give free expression to (a strong emotion): "he had come to **vent** his rage and despair"

Speak your pain. When we stop ourselves from feeling pain, we will return to the pain over and over again. Why not go all the way there, so you don't ever have to again? Acknowledge your feelings and your pain. Speak to it so you can start the healing process. Until the pain is acknowledged and dealt with, the hurt takes over and interferes with our attempts to heal.

How is this done? Contrary to what the perception might be, venting doesn't have to include screaming or ranting. One reason we don't vent is because it seems out of control or negative. Instead, if we can see letting out steam as an attempt to depressurize, it has a positive connotation. Venting is letting out what we have been holding in. Remember, in Chapter three, we discussed that feelings are normal and natural. It creates overwhelming pressure when we try to suppress or hold feelings inside. It is healthy to let them out. Perhaps you will write it out on a blank pad, type it on your computer, or say it out loud to yourself or a trusted friend. The goal is to name and validate the feelings. Be a witness to your pain and give voice to the feelings you have about the "it." Speak it to start the healing process.

Validation is a term used in many fields about accuracy and perspective. In the intelligence community, it is "a process associated with the collection and production of intelligence that confirms that an intelligence collection or production requirement is sufficiently important to justify the dedication of intelligence resources, does not duplicate an existing requirement, and has not been previously satisfied." Whew, that was a mouthful. In the military, it's "a part of target development that ensures all vetted targets meet the objectives and criteria outlined in the commander's guidance and ensures compliance with the law of armed conflict and rules of engagement." In computer modeling and simulation, it is "the process of determining the degree to which a model or simulation is an accurate representation of the real world from the perspective of the intended uses of the model or simulation."

The last one is intriguing— "an accurate representation of the real world from the perspective of the original intent." Original intent—wow, what an important thing to remember. Accuracy is measured by looking at the intention of its use or purpose. God's original plan for us was fellowship, love, peace, and freedom from all of the things we struggle with in the world. What was the original intention for our emotions? Because God made us in His image, our emotions are not a mistake. On the contrary, they are a gift from God. Emotions are a necessary and vital part of our worship. They are a vehicle for our connection with Him. The original intention would include our ability to enjoy Him, to worship Him, to be moved by what moves Him, and to experience love and compassion as He does.

We struggle because His original intention was interrupted by the human desire to be in control and to be the God for our own lives. Without understanding emotions as God-given, we can allow them to be infected and confused. God never intended for emotions to control us. When we acknowledge and validate them, they are a long-term gift to shift us out of the stuck cycle.

In psychological terms, validation is one way we communicate understanding and acceptance. It is the recognition and acceptance of another person's thoughts, feelings, sensations, and behaviors. Self-validation is the recognition and acceptance of your thoughts, feelings, sensations and behaviors as understandable and reasonable given the "it" that fueled them. It is important to note—validation does not mean agreement; it means acceptance. Self-validation is less accepted yet it is at the heart of *getting over*. God created within us a need to belong—to be accepted and known. While it is important from others, it is equally important to receive from and for ourselves.

When we validate an experience, it does not rule us or dictate our future responses. We are not giving power to "it." In actuality, validating steals power from "it" and transfers the power to us to move on.

This validation process includes allowing yourself to be angry about what is wrong; what was done; what you lost; what was taken; what you don't know; and what you cannot yet feel.

This step in the *getting over* process may need the most time. We cannot gloss over it or take it lightly. Often, we don't allow ourselves the time we need to integrate the validation of our experiences, along with the feelings and emotions that accompany them. We spend time and energy telling ourselves that what we feel is not valid. We minimize, deny, or ignore the feelings we have in response to the circumstances. We keep feelings in place when we ignore them. We bury them deeper when we deny them. They become entrenched/ fixed in place, and therefore, tough to remove.

We keep feelings in place when we ignore them. We bury them deeper when we deny them.

The look on someone's face when they hear, (perhaps for the first time), "you make sense," and "no wonder you are having such a hard time." The mix of curiosity and wonderment tends to be the basis for them to change as long as they can receive it. They can breathe when they hear, "you are not weird, crazy, or wrong to think this." The person feels "allowed" to understand and accept the feelings they've previously pushed aside or diminished. This step creates an opening for real growth.

Validation of the feeling closes the loop by connecting to the root cause instead of cycling in avoidance. Validation allows some closure. It says both, "I feel this way because" and "this happened, so I feel."

Psalm 37:5 (NIV)
"*Open up* before God, keep nothing back, He'll do whatever needs to be done. He'll *validate* your life in the clear light of day and stamp you with approval at high noon."

Acknowledge your anger, your pain, your trauma, and your heartache, then allow yourself to *feel* the weight of your emotions. Feelings are not good or bad in and of themselves. If you allow them to surface, they will not overwhelm you. In fact, by acknowledging them, you can exercise more control over them than if you ignore them. The purpose is to move through, not to lose yourself in the feeling and let them drive your life. The pushed aside and ignored feelings control you as much as when the emotions are front and center. The purpose of validating or venting is to gain a proper perspective on what the emotions are and learn a healthy way to process, and make decisions based on them. The decisions will tie to the *truths* you have been standing on. In that light, the truth you listen to is crucial. Will it be what you were taught in your home, or from some difficult experience or relationship? Or will you align your mind to God's truth, and believe what He says about you. This is a critical choice to make in order to have true freedom. Here are some verses that will tell you how God feels about you because true validation only comes from truth, the *Word of God*. Read through the following verses and take in God's truth about you.

"…in all these things we are more than conquerors through him who loved us." Romans 8:37 (NIV)

"But you are a chosen people, a royal priesthood, a holy nation, God's special possession, that you may declare the praises of him who called you out of darkness into his wonderful light." 1 Peter 2:9 (NIV)

"For we are God's handiwork, created in Christ Jesus to do good works, which God prepared in advance for us to do." Ephesians 2:10 (NIV)

"Now if we are children, then we are heirs- heirs of God and co-heirs with Christ. If indeed we share in His sufferings in order that we may also share with His glory." Romans 8:17 (NIV)

"What a God we have! And how fortunate we are to have him, this Father of our Master Jesus! Because Jesus was raised from the dead, we've been given a brand-new life and have everything to live for, including a future in heaven - and the future starts now!" (1 Peter 1:3-4 MSG)

"Oh yes, you shaped me first inside, then out; you formed me in my mother's womb. I thank you, High God—you're breathtaking! Body and soul, I am marvelously made! I worship in adoration—what a creation! You know me inside and out, you know every bone in my body; You know exactly how I was made, bit by bit, how I was sculpted from nothing into something. Like an open book, you watched me grow from conception to birth; all the stages of my life were spread out before you. The days of my life all prepared before I'd even lived one day." Psalm 139:13-16 (MSG)

"So, what do you think? With God on our side like this, how can we lose? If God didn't hesitate to put everything on the line for us, embracing our condition and exposing himself to the worst by sending His own Son, is there anything else he wouldn't gladly and freely do for us? And who would dare tangle with God by messing with one of God's chosen? Who would dare even to point a finger? The One who died for us—who was raised to life for us!— is in the presence of God at this very moment sticking up for us. Do you think anyone is going to be able to drive a wedge between us and Christ's love for us? There is no way! Not trouble, not hard times, not hatred, not hunger, not homelessness, not bullying threats, not backstabbing, not even the worst sins listed in Scripture:

They kill us in cold blood because they hate you. We're sitting ducks; they pick us off one by one. None of this fazes us because Jesus loves us. I'm absolutely convinced that nothing—nothing living or dead, angelic or demonic, today or tomorrow, high or low, thinkable or unthinkable—absolutely nothing can get between us and God's love because of the way that Jesus our Master has embraced us." Romans 8:31-39 The Message (MSG)

"This resurrection life you received from God is not a timid, grave-tending life. It's adventurously expectant, greeting God with a childlike "What's next, Papa?" God's Spirit touches our spirits and confirms who we really are. We know who he is, and we know who we are: Father and children. And we know we are going to get what's coming to us—an unbelievable inheritance! We go through exactly what Christ goes through. If we go through the hard times with him, then we're certainly going to go through the good times with him!" Romans 8:15-17 (MSG)

The ultimate validation comes from the Creator of the Universe who loves and accepts you and offers you eternal life through the sacrifice of His Son Jesus. Standing firm on this truth is the basis of a life free from the "it" you face.

Once we Vent and Validate the feelings, it is time to Verify them. Verify is defined: to establish truth, accuracy, or reality. More specifically, we verify our experience of each feeling and tie it back to the "it". Verify what happened and that it had impact in the form of feelings. We will deal with the response to your "it" in the next chapter. For now, it is important to verify that your feelings came from somewhere and have a real place in your life.

Verify your experience and how you feel about it. Create a sentence that sounds like, "I feel_____ because _____happened to me. I am stuck because I haven't given myself permission to understand what happened and to accept the feelings that I naturally have about it." (Again, this is not equal to the "feelings are everything," camp) Say it aloud and then use the all-important follow up phrases, which sound like this:

"No wonder."
"It makes sense."
"I make sense!"

Presenting the truth to yourself about your feelings allows light into the darkness. It frees you to understand yourself in light of your experience with your "it." Here are a few reminders about the truth of feelings:

- Feelings are just feelings—neither good or bad, right or wrong in themselves.

- It is justified to feel what you feel. (Remember this does not speak to the response to the feelings—we will look at that in the next chapter).

- You are not the only one who has these feelings or would have them in a similar experience.

- You can speak your feelings to illuminate them and disable the power they have previously had over you.

- You can live in the light of truth instead of the darkness of shame.

- You can turn on the lights! Confirm and substantiate your feelings.

"No wonder. It makes sense. I make sense." Say these words and take a deep breath. It's as if you've needed to say and hear those words to dislodge you from the stuck cycle. It gives fresh wind for your sails. You can now chart a course to the side of the *getting over* process that involves acting on the emotions. The E step directs you to your decisions about the emotions and your response to them. You can move now from the OV, the "scene of the crime," from the "it" to the E.R., the emergency room, where the wounds can be identified and treated. This marks the beginning of the second set of steps, a huge sign of progress in the *getting over* process. Take a moment to celebrate this hard work and then come back, so we can Evaluate, Embrace, Examine and Emerge.

EVALUATE YOUR INTERPRETATIONS

EMBRACE YOUR FEELINGS

EXAMINE YOUR OPTIONS - EMERGE IN TRUTH

EIGHT

ovEr: Evaluate /Embrace / Examine & Emerge

How Do You Want to Handle It?

"Those who do not run away from our pains but touch them with compassion bring healing and new strength. The paradox indeed is that the beginning of healing is in the solidarity with the pain."

— *Henri J.M. Nouwen*

The third step toward *getting over* is to Evaluate your interpretations, Embrace the feelings, Examine your options, and Emerge in Truth and new strength.

EVALUATE your interpretations:

When you have a feeling, what is the first thing you tell yourself about it? Do you hear one of the following phrases?

- I shouldn't feel that way.

- It's selfish to feel that.

- Someone else has it harder than I do.

- That's a sin.

- It won't matter what I feel anyway.

- This is overwhelming and I'm uncomfortable with these feelings.

The above are interpretations of your feelings. In chapters two and three, we learned that we get many of our interpretations from our childhood. It could have been a coach, a teacher, or a parent who shaped this interpretation. It may have been you in response to what you saw in these authority figures. Who or what is your interpreter when it comes to your feelings? Is it your parents and what they taught you about feelings? Is it early experiences with people who gave you the message it was wrong, dangerous, or uncomfortable to feel and express that feeling? Is it a culture that says it's not nice, cool or politically correct to feel that? Is it your mindset that tells you feelings make you weak? Is it your current mood, your background, or the circumstances you are facing?

In the book of Genesis, we read about Joseph, who as a young boy, had some experience with dreams and interpreting them. At a point later in his life when he was asked to interpret the dreams of two men, he had this to say:

"We had dreams," they said to him, "but there is no one to interpret them."
Then Joseph said to them, "Don't interpretations belong to God? Tell me your dreams."

Genesus 40:8 (HCSB)

When we interpret our feelings as wrong, bad, or unimportant, we push them back down and, in effect, intensify them while at the same time, we silence them. In this state, we have little power over the expression of our feelings and usually express them in undesirable ways. When we accept that feelings are God-given and not wrong, that He sent His Spirit to help us interpret them as such, we have a better chance of making mindful decisions about the actions we choose to take in response to them. First, we need to embrace our feelings as okay, important, and useful. Next, we need to *Evaluate* the Interpreter of our feelings. This is a great question to ask:

> "Are you interpreting your God through your life or your life through your God?"
>
> — Steven Furtick

EMBRACE your feelings:

"What? Are you kidding me?"

Okay, this step may make you think: I've tracked with you this far, but this is really too much. Maybe I can accept that my feelings about this are "okay," but how can you ask me to embrace them? I want to be over this annoying, horrible thing and now you're telling me to embrace it? In writing this chapter, I acknowledge this will feel counterintuitive. The last thing we want to do is figuratively cuddle close with the person, emotion or situation that hurt us or keeps us stuck. It is important to note, we are not embracing the person or the situation, but the feelings we have about the person or the situation.

For me, it conjures up all the alien horror movies I've seen, which I could probably list on one hand. I was deeply concerned about the green lady in the Wizard of Oz and thought the shark in Jaws was living and swimming in my pool. My much braver husband, a fan of the genre, encouraged me to watch a few after we married. You know the type—unsuspecting people confronted with a creature so frightening, so devastating, a threat to their very existence. The kind of people who know the ugly creature is around every corner. The whole movie you are on guard, holding your breath and waiting, knowing it will pop out at any moment and you'll let out an uncontrollable scream. (Or maybe that's just what I do.) The last thing you want are the characters to look for the ugly creature and invite it in. After all, aliens have a notorious reputation for doing terrible things once exposed or let loose on humanity. They especially seem to like to inhabit the bodies of humans and do all kinds of gross things (my psychological term) once living inside the victim. When the lead character goes to find the creature, we yell at the screen, "Don't go in there!" We think they are naïve or dumb or crazy to go toward the thing that can hurt them, but they do! (I'm still not a fan!)

God's original plan was something entirely different than what we are living. His intention for a relationship with His beloved children was perfection, order, peace, and love. With the entrance of sin in the world, everything broke—people, the planet, our genes, everything became less than what God intended for us. Our traumas, wounds, and painful experiences are like aliens living within us, taking over while we spend our lives running away or hiding to avoid the shock to our system if we encounter the monster. We run away from ourselves or block out or hide parts of ourselves in the process. We can't outrun our "it." It always catches up to us. The better goal is to acknowledge it, know where it is, and do what it takes to either remove it or keep it in a safe place.

You have a story, but you are not your story. Embrace the story that made you who you are, warts and all. It seems non-therapeutic, but in reality, it frees us to accept what is, rather than what we wish it was.

Here is another "old-fashioned" reference to a 1980s TV show and its very flashy star. His name on the show was B.A. Baracus. He was bigger than life with a tight Mohawk, huge biceps, and a slew of big gold chains around his neck. He was the "muscle" of the A-Team and quite intimidating. His real name is Mr. T. If this image doesn't work for you, think of any number of rappers or singers today with large gold chains around their necks. The chains we carry, in contrast, are not valuable or pleasing to the eye. They are heavy, imposing, labeled with our scars and experiences. They are the first thing someone sees. To embrace the chains does not mean we continue to carry the heaviness they offer. It means we acknowledge the labels they bear are a part of us. The things that happened made a difference and perhaps changed us in some way, but we get to choose what to do with the scars, the pain, and the power they possess. We objectify, validate, and then embrace this is part of my story, but it is not all of who I am or who I will become. Embrace the truth of the experience you went through. Disable the false power it has over you. Look at it in the eye, and then evaluate your choices going forward.

> **Embrace the truth of the experience you went through. Disable the false power it has over you.**

EXAMINE your options and **EMERGE** in Truth:

What is your choice? What will you do with this now that you have *Opened* and *Objectified*, *Validated* and *Vented*, *Evaluated* and *Embraced*? Next comes the step of *Examining* your options.

This examination includes the knowledge that you always have options. This concept is foreign to many. They feel powerless and hopeless thinking, they "have to" feel and do based on some set of conditions. They feel stuck and act out of obligation and habit, instead of the freedom that comes with knowing and examining the options. Resentment arises when we are unaware that we have them. If you feel resentful, or worse, bitter; chances are excellent you don't believe you have any options. Believing options exist is the first step. The second step is believing we have the power to act upon them. We have power when we realize we can make a new choice at every exchange. It is freeing to weigh options and make informed choices. Looking at and weighing options is important for understanding the power we have in any situation. We have choices, but to be able to make informed choices, we have to evaluate the options—both good and bad ones.

An important option to consider in this step is forgiveness. Forgiveness is often misunderstood to mean acceptance or reconciliation. It doesn't, however, mean a reconciled relationship or reestablishment of trust with the one who hurt you. Forgiveness is between you and God; an act of obedience and a step of faith. When we extend forgiveness, we effectively give God the outcome and trust Him with what may feel like our need to get even or to be made whole. Forgiveness is one person's choice. Reconciliation requires two people acting in a way that allows for peace and the relationship to thrive. It is still our responsibility to forgive even without reconciliation because doing so offers true freedom from holding onto the debts they *owed* us. The debts are crushing and impossible to carry.

> Romans 12:18 says, "If it is possible, as far as it depends on you, live at peace with everyone." (NIV)

This verse tells me it is not always possible to live in peace with everyone, and it is not only up to me. As a visual person, I picture a fence separating two green pastures. It is up to us to move forward to the fence. It is our job to do what we can to get there and to stay there. We cannot drag someone to our side of the fence or do the work for them. You may say, "That's not fair! I'm the only one doing anything and they are the one who did something wrong!" The verse that follows helps with that.

"Do not take revenge, my dear friends, but leave room for God's wrath, for it is written: "It is mine to avenge; I will repay," says the Lord. On the contrary: "If your enemy is hungry, feed him; if he is thirsty, give him something to drink. In doing this, you will heap burning coals on his head.

Do not be overcome by evil, but overcome evil with good."
Romans 8:19-21 (NIV)

We also have the option to forgive ourselves. It may sound counterintuitive or downright wrong, but it's a necessary step to choose if we are to *Emerge* from our "it" with the truth. Forgive yourself for believing the lie; for holding the anger; for coping and not dealing; for allowing others to have power over you; for not having boundaries and so on. Free yourself. You were not responsible or at fault. Clear the decks for truth. This is in no way about taking responsibility for what you could not control as a child, or for what you believed as a result, but for the time when you *were* able to do something differently but were stuck. This is an exercise about freeing yourself from holding on to self-recrimination or guilt. It allows you to make way for the truth to take hold.

To Emerge from your "it," there are some important reminders:

- It is important to separate people's opinions from God's truth. When in doubt, check it against the Word of God, see what He says and follow that.

- Remember, we don't rise or fall on the approval or opinions of people.

- Listen carefully to God's voice. The closer you listen, the more you will hear.

- God alone gives you purpose and when we trust that, we allow Him to direct our path and make it straight.

- No joke, this is strange but true, a bit like keeping your friends close and your enemies closer. Know your "it" and where you are vulnerable so you can prepare for "it" resurfacing.

- Take every thought, both negative and positive captive in obedience to Christ. Our thoughts inform our feelings, so this is a crucial step.

We *objectify* the experience, *validate* and *verify* that the feelings are real and this in turn gives information from which we are can *evaluate* and *examine* new choices. The victories come when we *renew* our minds in the process of our transformation. Let's move on to the final step!

RELEASE
RESPOND
REBUILD

NINE

oveR: Release/Respond/Rebuild

What Will This Mean Going Forward?

"A sum can be put right: but only by going back till you find the error and working it afresh from that point, never by simply going on."

— C.S. Lewis, The Great Divorce

"Whether you say you can't or you can, you're right."

— Walt Disney Company

'm not much of a hang glider. Okay, I'm not a hang glider at all! I imagine it is exhilarating and exciting to be soaring through the air taking in all of the scenery from a vantage point you couldn't have otherwise. From what I read, I understand hang gliding is about focus. To be exact, what a hang glider focuses on is where he will end up. What the eye looks to is where the glider goes.

Remember the questions I ask of clients when they are in the first session? "What brings you here?" and "What do you want from the time we spend together?" The latter question is about setting the destination point and focusing on it as we move through the process of *getting OVER*. The final step is about the end goal and where you place your focus. What would it look like for you to release your "it", the power it has had to keep you "stuck," and to focus on where you are going rather than where you have been. The steps involved are all action verbs and involve choice and a response.

RELEASE

To reach for the new, you have to *release* the old. A trapeze artist needs to release his current bar to swing out to the new bar or he loses momentum and must either return to the starting point, or drop to the net below. It may take several practice swings to learn to swing out far enough to grab the bar. He may have to risk the fall to release the bar. Similarly, in order to move from one place to another, we must leave and go. There is risk involved in the release. But remember, you have a built-in net that will support you in case of a fall. To fly, we have to let it go. (Oh no, that song again, sorry!) Once you work through the steps that lead to this one, you are ready to focus on what is ahead, not what was before. You can release the old and move to the new.

RESPOND

What will your *response* be to the situations in your life? On his way to Jerusalem, the apostle Paul faced an unknown and potentially dangerous situation. He spoke of the reason he chose to respond in the way he did, and we can read about that in the book of Acts.

"But there is another urgency before me now. I feel compelled to go to Jerusalem. I'm completely in the dark about what will happen when I get there. I do know that it won't be any picnic, for the Holy Spirit has let me know repeatedly and clearly that there are hard times and imprisonment ahead. But that matters little. What matters most to me is to finish what God started: the job the Master Jesus gave me of letting everyone I meet know all about this incredibly extravagant generosity of God."

Acts 20:22-24 The Message (MSG)

"So how am I to respond? I've decided that I really don't care about their motives, whether mixed, bad, or indifferent. Every time one of them opens his mouth, Christ is proclaimed, so I just cheer them on!

And I'm going to keep that celebration going because I know how it's going to turn out. Through your faithful prayers and the generous response of the Spirit of Jesus Christ, everything he wants to do in and through me will be done. I can hardly wait to continue on my course. I don't expect to be embarrassed in the least. On the contrary, everything happening to me in this jail only serves to make Christ more accurately known, regardless of whether I live or die. They didn't shut me up; they gave me a pulpit! Alive, I'm Christ's messenger; dead, I'm his bounty. Life versus even more life! I can't lose."

Philippians 1:18-21 (MSG)

Paul was a rejoicer—he actively chose this posture even as he acknowledged being "completely in the dark" about what would happen to him. He did know his course would not be easy, yet he chose to look to God and trust Him with his life. He chose to rejoice, a voluntary position. It's something we can also choose. True joy is related to how we value God, and the voluntary choice we make to trust Him.

Respond by choosing to live in the truth—no longer listen to and respond to the lies of the past. Will you jump this hurdle and get to the other side or stay stuck? You get to choose! Maybe you didn't get to choose what has come your way, but the response is yours.

"You can't go back and change the beginning, but you can start where you are and change the ending" C.S. Lewis.

The Bible is full of redemption stories, with rocky or downright tragic starts. God has a way of making of these seemingly implausible stories turn out in ways no one would have imagined. Romans eight speaks of this redemption— we are not stuck in our struggles—we are sanctified, conformed into the image of Christ. Our redemption story is progressing, and the ending will blow our minds. Christ is our Redeemer—the Writer of our story and He weaves every experience of our lives into our story. The founder of Alcoholics Anonymous said, "Nothing is wasted in God's economy."

The Bible says it this way:

"God is able to orchestrate everything to work toward something good and beautiful when we love him and accept his invitation to live according to his plan."

Romans 8:28 (THE VOICE)

You can't change who wasn't there for you, what hurt you, what they said, or how it felt. You can decide it will be for good in your life because God said so. He will finish what He started in you. With that knowledge, you can tell your "it": "This stops here. You are done."

REBUILD

Renew and Restore

"Do not conform to the pattern of this world, but be transformed by the *renewing* of your mind. Then you will be able to test and approve what God's will is—his good, pleasing and perfect will."

Romans 12:2 New International Version (NIV)

"Not that I have already obtained this or am already perfect, but I press on to make it my own, because Christ Jesus has made me his own. Brothers, I do not consider that I have made it my own. But one thing I do: forgetting what lies behind and straining forward to what lies ahead, I press on toward the goal for the prize of the upward call of God in Christ Jesus."

Philipians 3:12-14 (NIV)

Place Your Life Before God

"So here's what I want you to do, God helping you: Take your everyday, ordinary life—your sleeping, eating, going-to-work, and walking-around life—and place it before God as an offering. Embracing what God does for you is the best thing you can do for him. Don't become so well-adjusted to your culture that you fit into it without even thinking. Instead, fix your attention on God. You'll be changed from the inside out. Readily recognize what he wants from you, and quickly respond to it. Unlike the culture around you, always dragging you down to its level of immaturity, God brings the best out of you, develops well-formed maturity in you."

Romans 12:1-2 The Message (MSG)

85

The battle is in the mind. There is a direct connection between your perspective and your eventual response. Our thoughts in the natural battle or resist the knowledge of God. They are tied up in all kinds of misperceptions, and only God's Truth corrects the errors of perspective in our minds. It is the interpretation of events that create the response more than the events themselves. When we take our thoughts captive and challenge our perspective, we are able to lay them down in favor of God's truth. We can choose to see His plan and take courage in the most difficult of circumstances. A correct interpretation represents our power to see the situation clearly and decide what we will do from that point forward.

Only God's Truth corrects the errors of perspective in our minds.

"We demolish arguments and every pretension that sets itself up against the knowledge of God, and we take captive every thought to make it obedient to Christ."

2 Corinthians 10:5 (NIV)

Have you ever seen the mosaic artwork that looks like one thing from a distance, but when you look closer, it is made up of thousands of smaller pictures or dots? You can lose sight of the bigger picture if you focus in on a smaller one. Perspective is very important when dealing with our thoughts. Zoom out. It's a helpful reminder that sometimes we are so focused on something we cannot see anything but that focal point. When we zoom out and see the issue from a higher vantage point, we can see more and better with a new perspective.

Joyce Meyer wrote: "Many people will be on their way to heaven but won't enjoy the trip." Many don't understand how to live in the fullness Christ came to give, and the power of the Holy Spirit within them. We hear about this power but can't believe it could be possible for us to have or to use effectively.

I recently read this powerful post from Pastor Mitch Horton that described this power and how to use it:

"Authority is delegated power. A person's authority exceeds his personal strength! As a believer, you have been given the authority of the kingdom of heaven; the actual authority that Jesus has over Satan to deal with him and his onslaughts in your life! God knew that you needed a weapon of defense and offense when He redeemed you and left you in a fallen world with a malevolent enemy that seeks to harm you and your family. This authority enables you to send Satan on the run before he harms your family. Christians have access to the "badge" of authority in the use of the name of Jesus! Jesus has given us the unqualified use of His name in His absence. His NAME represents His person, His position, His seating, and His authority! "If you ask (demand) anything in my name, I will do it" (John 14:14). Jesus' name will accomplish everything that He can without Him personally being present! "Most assuredly, I say to you, he who believes in me, the works that I do will he do also; and greater works than these he will do, because I go to the Father" (John 14:12). His name is above every name! Every demon force must bow to the name JESUS! (See Philippians 2:9-11).

You have been given AUTHORITY that is far greater than your natural strength.

To do nothing about it, or to whine and complain about how bad things are will only give Satan control over you! That would be like the police officer laying down in the street and crying because a vehicle refused to obey his instructions! He has to enforce the law and sometimes that means forcing people to submit to what they know is right! Satan is the same way. If you lie down and do nothing when attacked, He will dominate you. That's what most believers do today!

*When confronted with financial lack, oppression, depres-
sion, fear, weakness, failure, or anything else that steals, kills,
and destroys, RISE UP IN THE NAME OF JESUS AND
COMMAND SATAN'S POWER TO BE BROKEN OVER
YOUR LIFE AND FAMILY! No one has more authority in
your life and family than you do!*

*Remember that we overcome by "the blood of the Lamb," and
by the "word of our testimony,"(Rev. 12:11) and by the use of
the Name of Jesus. Because of Jesus, we are already made "more
than conquerors"(Romans 8:37)!"*

By Pastor Mitch Horton | August 2003 |

There's more to life than this life. It's not just for you that
you do this work. You need to be *getting over it* for others
as well.

For not one of us lives for himself, and not one dies for
himself; [8] for if we live, we live for the Lord, or if we die,
we die for the Lord; therefore whether we live or die, we
are the Lord's.

Romans 14:7-9 (NASB)

To glorify God with our lives and have the capacity to
help others, sometimes we first have to move our "self" out
of the way. When we are stuck,
the focus is clearly on me, that
makes it almost impossible
to see anyone *other than* me.
Although this *getting over* process is about moving past that
which holds us back, hurts us
or has traumatized us, it is also intended to move us to a point
where we can help others find the same freedom we found.
We do this step: Release, Respond, Rebuild—to move the

> **To glorify God with our lives and have the capacity to help others, sometimes we first have to move our "self" out of the way.**

self as the focal point to God as the focus, so we can see His purpose for us and move forward into it.

"All praise to the God and Father of our Master, Jesus the Messiah! Father of all mercy! God of all healing counsel! He comes alongside us when we go through hard times, and before you know it, he brings us alongside someone else who is going through hard times so that we can be there for that person just as God was there for us. We have plenty of hard times that come from following the Messiah, but no more so than the good times of his healing comfort—we get a full measure of that, too."

2 Corinthians 1:3-5 (MSG)

"But we do not belong to those who shrink back and are destroyed, but to those who have faith and are saved."

Hebrews 10:39 New International Version (NIV)

"So let's keep focused on that goal, those of us who want everything God has for us. If any of you have something else in mind, something less than total commitment, God will clear your blurred vision—you'll see it yet! Now that we're on the right track, let's stay on it. Stick with me, friends. Keep track of those you see running this same course, headed for this same goal. There are many out there taking other paths, choosing other goals, and trying to get you to go along with them. I've warned you of them many times; sadly, I'm having to do it again. All they want is easy street. They hate Christ's Cross. But easy street is a dead-end street. Those who live there make their bellies their gods; belches are their praise; all they can think of is their appetites. But there's far more to life for us. We're citizens of high heaven! We're waiting the arrival of the Savior, the Master, Jesus Christ, who will transform our earthy bodies into glorious bodies like his own. He'll make us beautiful and whole with the same powerful skill by which he is putting everything as it should be, under and around him."

Philippians 3:15-21 MSG

I love the descriptive nature of that verse! There is no position more glorious than being called sons and daughters of God. Remember this position and you will be able to focus on the your purpose and encounter His restoration.

Restore

"Then I will (restore) make up to you for the years that the swarming locust has eaten, The creeping locust, the stripping locust and the gnawing locust, My great army which I sent among you." Joel 2:25 NASB

We don't hear that much about locusts these days. For most of us, we may have heard stories of them swarming in huge numbers, blocking out the sun and ravaging fields and trees and everything else they touched. It's not normal for the average person to run across a locust, much less to encounter a swarm of them. According to the USDA, locusts are *voracious* eaters, and not picky about their meal plan! They are a type of grasshopper, but their behavior sets them apart. Locusts can exist alone, but under certain circumstances, they can also migrate and swarm. "A Desert Locust adult can consume roughly its own weight in fresh food per day, that is about two grams every day. A one km size swarm contains about 40 million locusts, which eat the same amount of food in one day as about 35,000 people, 20 camels or six elephants..."

Locusts devour everything of value in their path. They are indiscriminate. Our "it" can feel like that, like locusts eating away at us. The "locusts" in your life stand to devour all your hard work, your plans for the future, your peace, health, and wellbeing. For a season, it may feel that your "it" may have succeeded, but God is a God who restores. The passage speaks to God's judgment and His goodness. He must judge sin, but He is always offering restoration and redemption. When God restores, it is a full restoration, beyond what we can even imagine. It may not be a restoration of things, but instead of His presence and our relationship with Him. The process of restoration offers at least two important outcomes:

- A deepened fellowship with God

"The tested genuineness of your faith − more precious than gold that perishes though it is tested by fire may result in praise and glory and honor at the revelation of Jesus Christ."

1 Peter 1:7 (ESV)

God's goal is to restore us to His original intent for our lives. The plan was for His creation to bring glory to His name, to reflect His glory with our lives. His plan of redemption in love is to bring us back to Himself, the Author and Creator. He loves us enough to offer us true fellowship with Him. As the psalmist says,

"You make known to me the path of life; in your presence there is fullness of joy, in your right hand are pleasures for evermore."

Psalm 16:11 (ESV)

The process of going through trials and difficulties bring to light the need for us to trust Him and the opportunity to deepen our fellowship with Him. We grow deeper in our fellowship with Him when we choose to believe in His goodness and mercy, to know He will never leave or forsake us despite the "it" we face.

- A long term gain.

"You shall eat in plenty and be satisfied, and praise the name of the Lord your God, who has dealt wondrously with you. And my people shall never again be put to shame. You shall know that I am in the midst of Israel, and that I am the LORD your God and there is none else. And my people shall never again be put to shame."

Joel 2:26-27 (NRSV)

Gil's Exposition of the Bible explains the verse this way:

"they shall not be ashamed of their faith and hope, and expectation of good things promised them; nor of the word and ordinances, and the profession they have made of Christ in this world; nor shall they be ashamed at his coming; but shall be placed at his right hand, and received into his kingdom, and shall be led by him to fountains of living water, and be satisfied with pleasures for evermore."

God is in the business of restoring us every day, of making all things new. He wants to take you from the devastation of your "it" eating away at you to full restoration. Whereas redemption requires a redeemer, restoration is a reciprocal act. He chose us, and we choose to surrender to Him. We are in the process of restoration when we celebrate the knowledge, He is the Lord our God, and there is none else. We can withstand the storms of life when we know He is on our side and His promises, or as I like to call them, His *rainbows*, are true.

TEN

The Song Within The Storm
Reading Rainbows

"We are not responsible for the circumstances we are in, but we are responsible for the way we allow those circumstances to affect us; we can either allow them to get on top of us or we can sallow them to transform us into what God wants us to be."
— *Oswald Chambers*

"Life isn't about waiting for the storm to pass...It's about learning to dance in the rain."
— *Vivian Greene*

"Where there is ruin, there is hope for treasure."
— *Rumi*

There is something so wondrous about seeing a rainbow in the sky after a rainstorm just as the sun starts to peek out. Rainbows make us stop and look; they make us smile. We take pictures and post them. We point at them and show others to make sure they don't miss the special sighting. If you have ever seen a double rainbow, it feels like you just won the lottery! Did you know that rainbows can be in the sky but are not visible? Or that rainbows can be present at night and lit by the moonlight? We definitely know when we see a rainbow, but seeing a rainbow and reading one are two different things.

A rainbow is sunshine on rain. The rainbow and rain are the same distance away. How interesting that the rain reflects the rainbow. The rain is a necessary part of the rainbow. It takes what some see as a bad thing (rain) to make what is a good thing (rainbow). They happen at the same time! It is easy to think we can only find the good once the bad is over. We get stuck waiting for the rain to stop, or asking why it is raining in the first place. We believe the only time the rainbow can happen is after rain. But rainbows happen *because* of the rain and are visible through the water in the atmosphere. We read a rainbow when we see life's storms as lessons and experiences that we have the power to get past. Rainbows represent a promise of God. His promises are everywhere, and it is our job to read them even when they don't seem to be there. We can choose to see the promises of God in the middle of the storms we face even if we don't know how our "it" could be good. He promises that He is working it all out and it will be for our benefit.

"Get over it!" By now, I hope you hear those three little words in a totally different way, no longer as an angry rant, but perhaps now as a rainbow. Perhaps you can now hear it as a statement of encouragement and hope. Maybe it fosters a determination to move on from what has kept you stuck. Now maybe it sounds like a promise of God that says, "Yes, you *can* be free from this." There is a progression of that phrase that goes like this:

Speak it
Feel it

Choose it
Do it

Or maybe like this:

Get it out
Get into it
Get to it
Get through it
Give it over

...and once clearly understood, the phrase says, "Get over it!":

- and stay married

- and get healthy

- and be happy/choose joy

- and manage anxiety/fear

Jesus spoke to sickness and storms and told us to speak to the figurative mountains standing in our way. He was illustrating the power of faith. His power to rescue is bigger than any of our shifting circumstances. We can use His power to speak to our "its". You have a voice, the power to read the rainbows and speak to your mountains. Speak these powerful phrases as a start:

- "God alone gave me my purpose, and God alone will approve my path."

- "I won't rise from the approval of people, and I won't fall from the lack of it."

- "I must separate people's opinions from God's truth."

- "I will seek the applause of God and not the approval of people."

- "I will let God's voice be my authority."

- "It's not where I started, but where I choose to end up."

- "God can change in an instant what I can't in a lifetime."

- "God promises if I draw near to Him, He will draw near to me."

- "I can hold fast to the confession of my hope in Jesus."

- "I can stick together in community with people who will lovingly help me."

"So let's do it—full of belief, confident that we're presentable inside and out. Let's keep a firm grip on the promises that keep us going. He always keeps his word. Let's see how inventive we can be in encouraging love and helping out, not avoiding worshiping together as some do but spurring each other on, especially as we see the big Day approaching.

The Spirit of God, the Master, is on me because God anointed me. He sent me to preach good news to the poor, heal the heartbroken, Announce freedom to all captives, pardon all prisoners."

Hebrews 10:22-25 (MSG)

"The Spirit of the Sovereign Lord is on me,
because the Lord has anointed me
to proclaim good news to the poor.
He has sent me to bind up the brokenhearted,
to proclaim freedom for the captives
and release from darkness for the prisoners."

Isaiah 61:1 (NIV)

"It is for freedom that Christ has set us free. Stand firm, then, and do not let yourselves be burdened again by a yoke of slavery."

Galatians 5:1 (NIV)

Let's review the four steps to see what has been taught so far:

Open up; Observe; Objectify
Vent; Validate; Verify
Evaluate; Embrace; Examine & Emerge
Release; Renew; Rebuild

"The teacher is always quiet during the test." This anonymous quote is profound in its message. We have all have taken more tests than we want to remember. We can recount endless hours listening to the teacher talk, preparing and stressing, maybe pulling all-nighters to try to pound the information into our brains. What may not be so memorable is the teacher sitting quietly during the test. They did their instructional job; it was now time for the students to use what they learned. The teacher remained in the room but didn't lead during the test. Similarly, it is our opportunity to use what God has taught us even when we think He is not there or He is silent. Though we may not be able to hear Him or understand His purpose in our circumstance, we can read His rainbows by remembering His promises. God used a rainbow to show Himself and to give hope and peace. Reading rainbows is a choice to see them even when they are not apparent or full. We can release, renew, and rebuild by trusting His promises are true. He promises we can do this through Him.

> Though we may not be able to hear Him or understand His purpose in our circumstance, we can read His rainbows by remembering His promises.

"I can do all things through Christ who strengthens me."

Philippians 4:13 (NIV)

Not some, or one, but *all* things, through Him.

"Anything that annoys you is for teaching you patience.
Anyone who abandons you is for teaching you how to stand on
your own two feet.
Anything that angers you is for teaching you forgiveness and
compassion.
Anything that has power over you is for teaching you how to
take your power back.
Anything you hate is for teaching you unconditional love.
Anything you fear is for teaching you courage to overcome your
fear.
Anything you can't control is for teaching you how to let go and
trust the Universe."

Jackson Kiddard

I graciously recommend a substitution for the word "universe" in that beautiful prose. My version would read, *"Let go and trust (the God of) the Universe,"* for He is the strength within us to take any action toward health and growth. He alone is the reason we can handle the difficult things that happen to us. He is the hope we have of salvation and eternity. A relationship with Jesus Christ offers us peace, stability, courage, love, strength, joy, and power. No matter what has you stuck, or how long you have been in that position, freedom is possible. When we trust God and bring our "it" to Him, we are truly able to get OVER!

SECTION THREE

Living Life Unstuck

ELEVEN

OVER: Faulty Foundations

"If we abandon the past in the pursuit of the future, we've left all of the construction materials behind. So, we might show up at the site, but we're not going to be building anything."
— *Craig D. Lounsbrough*

What's your family factor? How would you describe your home life? As we discussed in Chapter two, we all build on faulty foundations of a cracked and broken world based on where you originated. What are your relationships like with yourself and with others? If you are a parent, what will you show your children? What are your beliefs and behaviors?

I apologize in advance for the alliteration that is about to follow—you know, where the first letter of the each of the words are all the same?

Allow me to offer you a formula to consider:

Formula: Your foundation teaches you to function, which forecasts your future.

Foundation

The foundation of a home is what it sits on. It is the most critical part of the building structure. Any mistakes in the foundation will get worse the more the house is built. It is called "compounding defects." Whether the foundation is not squared properly or weakens with improper preparation, the foundational issues create significant problems. Your foundational experience is the same because it is made up of what you saw, assumed, and learned. Your personality impacts your foundation, too. Your family built with the tools they knew. Every family has faults in the foundation because they could only give from what they knew. If they were never taught, ("unless the Lord builds the house…you get a shack" Psalm 127:1) they were sure to build in compounding defects. As a result, your foundation is a bit shaky, weak, and not level. It is faulty. As firm as the concrete in the foundation of a house, so are the "teachings" of your childhood. You assume those foundational messages are correct because it's what you knew. We know all of our good and bad experiences as normal. This is how *home* feels. We're comfortable with it because it is familiar.

The goal goes beyond recognizing there are mistakes. While this is important in the over process, we need to name the mistakes. What are your faulty foundational bricks or beliefs? Maybe it's a belief that says:

- I must be happy all the time.

- My appearance is my identity.

- I need to make others happy or not make them mad.

- I can never show emotion.

- I have to take care of or make mom and dad okay.

- I have to keep quiet because we don't talk about that.

- I have to protect the family image.

- I must be perfect.

- I have to perform to earn love.

- I am only worthy if...

- I'm not lovable.

- I'm a burden.

- I'm just not _____ enough (fill in the blank),

- I can't say no because that would be mean.

- I need to control everything.

The above are common misconceptions that cause great disruption if we believe them. All of these broken and faulty bricks will cause relationship issues, consciously, or subconsciously. You need to do an inventory to bring them to the surface. Let's take a moment to put a name on each of those bad bricks. Make a list—don't edit yourself, just put down whatever comes to your mind.

What are your faulty bricks?

-

-

-

-

-

Function

We alter our personalities and form our identities in an attempt to find and keep stability. How do you function? What you believe influences how you behave. If you think you need to make everyone happy, you become a people pleaser. We go around reading everyone and contorting our feelings and responses to get their approval, real or perceived.

We may display these behaviors in our attempt to get along in the world: people-pleasing, lack of boundaries, seeking approval, shame, anxiety, eating disorders, addiction, relational distress, fear of failure, anger, discouragement, and insecurity.

Forecast/Future

The longer the foundation sets, the harder it is to break free from it. We continue to behave based on what we learned. Those repeated responses set like concrete. This, however, does not represent freedom in the present, but a reaction to the past. Our foundation teaches us to function, which will be a forecast of our future if not interrupted.

- If overprotected, we might become anxious trying to control or fear doing anything.

- If criticized, we might become a critic.

- If walked on or picked on, we might overcompensate with extreme toughness.

- If told feelings are wrong, we might have no ability to identify or process feelings.

- If silenced, we might not express appropriately, or at all.

- If we have no voice, we might act out in rebellion/rage.

What you stand on is what you believe. It determines how you behave, which sets your course and informs your outcomes. If you want to know what you are standing on, work backward at the current results of your life. Someone may have brought to your attention a remark about your short temper, critical outlook, or lack of communication skills. How you handle your emotions shows what you

What you stand on is what you believe. It determines how you behave, which sets your course and informs your outcomes.

believe. For example, if you struggle with anger, you may have been taught anger is wrong. If you struggle with control, you may have experienced chaos and believe you can only survive if your life isn't chaotic. The enemy wants you to stay on bad bricks, clueless. A big step to freedom is identifying the bad bricks.

This may be a difficult challenge to face this truth: it is okay and even important to experience and express your feelings. You are allowed to be sad or mad. You are right to feel hurt and anger. The emotional release will allow you to act as you move forward appropriately. If you aren't happy with the current outcomes of your relationships and you wonder, "Why do I keep dealing with this over and over?", check your foundation. Decide to recognize, embrace, and feel the effects of your "it" and then decide your next step. (The "it" is often the place where we get stuck trying to jump from knowledge to action without letting the heart respond.)

We have a living *hope* in Christ who came to set us free from this bondage. He promises that we can move on from our past and change the bad bricks for healthy, strong ones. You can believe and stand-on these truths:

- You are Lovable …

"This is how much God loved the world: He gave his Son, his one and only Son. And this is why: so that no one need be destroyed; by believing in him, anyone can have a whole and lasting life." John 3:16 MSG

- You are Acceptable...

"Christ arrives right on time to make this happen. He didn't, and doesn't, wait for us to get ready. He presented himself for this sacrificial death when we were far too weak and rebellious to do anything to get ourselves ready. And even if we hadn't been so weak, we wouldn't have known what to do anyway." Romans 5:8 (MSG) 6-8

- You are Capable...

"I can do all this through him who gives me strength." Philippians 4:13 NIV

- You are Forgivable...

"With the arrival of Jesus, the Messiah, that fateful dilemma is resolved. Those who enter into Christ's being-here-for-us no longer have to live under a continuous, low-lying black cloud." Romans 8:1-7 (MSG)

When you stand on these bricks as your foundation, you can see and choose and live in freedom, knowing you are standing on a firm foundation.

God is the builder, and He is in the business of rebuilding. We all need it. We can change out the old battery and connect to the source. Let Him heal you because you can't give others what you don't have. The pattern of your past will continue until you create a new pattern.

To summarize, we are broken. While we can't outlive family patterns or pathologies, we can take action to live beyond them. With God's help, we can change the direction of our present and future. This is the very message of the Bible: redemption, and grace.

Let's go back to that identity question. Who am I? The better question is: "Who does God say I am?" You *matter* to God, and it matters that you answer the question, or your past will try to answer it for you. The best thing we can do about our past whether it's a pebble in the road you keep stubbing your toe on or it's a solid wall that you can't see beyond; whether you have people-pleasing tendencies you are dealing with, or you are completely immobilized by fear; wherever you are on the continuum it is important to answer that question. Who does God say I am?

Here is an example of the *getting over* process applied to faulty foundations:

O – I am a people-pleaser and am living in a state of exhaustion. As a result, I cannot seem to keep up with all of the expectations of others. I learned to do this when my parents divorced, and my dad never came back.

V – I feel scared all the time and lost trying to meet the needs of others, so I am not abandoned again.

E – I acknowledge my feelings and know they are normal. I examine my options related to continuing in this way or starting to live a more authentic life.

R – I respond in the truth that I am loved by God and can release the lie that I must make others happy to earn their presence. I trust His will never leave me and rebuild my life around that belief.

If we can move these things into our awareness (know where you came from), and work to change where they are faulty and a hindrance (step off the faulty bricks), imagine what type of offering we can give—a healthy self, healthy relationships, and healthy families.

TWELVE

OVER: Anxiety

"Worrying is carrying tomorrow's load with today's strength-carrying two days at once. It is moving into tomorrow ahead of time. Worrying doesn't empty tomorrow of its sorrow, it empties today of its strength."

— *Corrie Ten Boom*

Lately, almost every new client I see struggles with some form of anxiety, especially young men and women over the past five years. Nearly every session is layered with anxiety or different symptoms of anxiety.

It has been said that what we fear we create. And it seems we have many fears. A 2014 Gallup poll listed terrorism, immigration, the size and power of the government, the economy, and healthcare among the top results of what people worry. While these are genuine concerns in our world today, the majority of what we fear lies in the unknown.

Consider these quotes on worry and anxiety:

"My life has been filled with terrible misfortune; most of which never happened."
— *Michel de Montaigne*

"If you see ten troubles coming down the road, you can be sure that nine will run into the ditch before they reach you."
— *Calvin Coolidge*

"When I look back on all these worries, I remember the story of the old man who said on his deathbed that he had had a lot of trouble in his life, most of which had never happened."
— *Winston Churchill*

"Barring serious accidents, if you are not preoccupied with worry and you work hard, you can look forward to a reasonably lengthy existence. It's not the hard work that kills; it's the worrying that kills."
— *Thomas Edison*

According to these quotes, and in my experience, we have quite an imbalance—lots of fear with little quantifiable reason for it. I have heard it said that 85% of what we fear never happens. Most of our worries are self-punishing exaggerations and misperceptions. You may have heard about the physiological problems a worried or anxious mind experiences. Chronic stress to the brain releases stress hormones that can lead to heart disease, cancer, depression, premature aging, marital and relational dysfunction.

Anxiety asks the big, scary question, "What if?" It is like a dark grey balloon that is launched and hovers overhead. Anxiety likes company and more "What if" balloons mean darkness and a lack of clarity. It's as if they are the "gloom, despair and agony" brigade blocking out any hope or help. It reminds me of an old song from a show called Hee-Haw. It went like this:

Gloom, despair, and agony on me
Deep, dark depression, excessive misery
If it weren't for bad luck, I'd have no luck at all
Gloom, despair, and agony on me
("Gloom, Despair and Agony on Me" from the TV Show "Hee-Haw" 1969 -1992) Buck Owens & Roy Clark)

An abundance of anxiety balloons leaves us feeling like the words of the song. We can also look at anxiety like a top. It cannot stand alone, and it requires help to start spinning and keep spinning. The rotational inertia keeps it in place once it is going until it is bumped off course or the spinning stops. When we turn the tops of "What if," we get wound so tight we cannot see straight.

Anxiety and control are linked. We are under the illusion that we are in control because we have instant access to all the answers we could ever want through a simple internet search. The digital age allows for all things to be "controlled" through one device: our calendar, communication, banking, shopping, our personal information, etc. We are instantly gratified by how quickly we can handle or control things. Just misplace your phone though—see how in control you feel then. Control is tenuous and elusive. The loss of control is always a source of fear, but once we understand we can only control ourselves, an opportunity for change arises.

To deal with anxiety effectively, we must answer the "What if" question fueling it. When we respond, with a "Then I will" to that anxiety question, we pop the balloon.

To deal with anxiety effectively, we must answer the "What if" question fueling it.

As a spinning top quickly falls off its axis with the slightest movement, if we can interrupt the anxious thoughts at the base, they fall, and the spinning stops. Our job is to "stop the top" by refocusing our minds. The antidote to anxiety is thanksgiving and gratitude because it sets our focus on what is real and right rather than the wrong or unknown.

As we discussed in Chapter one, one of the things that keep us stuck is our desire to know why. The same stagnate, unmotivating, and sometimes condemning question arises with anxiety. "Why?" The better question or questions begin with the word "what." The more productive questions are: "What's next?" Or, "What are my options?"

Here is an example of the OVER process applied to anxiety:

O : What happened? (Car accident, bad grade, fear of disappointing, out of control.)

V : I'm feeling anxious, nervous, upset, fearful. (Makes sense based on what happened.)

E : It's okay to feel anxious, I feel what I feel, what do I want to do with the feelings. (I have a choice.)

R : Respond in the truth—Release the lie. (What I am worried about is not likely to happen, and if it does, then I will trust that God is in control of my life and He will help me—I can trust Him and myself.)

THIRTEEN

OVER: Guilt and Shame

"Shame is a soul-eating emotion."

— *Carl Gustav Jung*

When you live with guilt, you will feel the punishment that comes with it. You may even look for it to validate what you believe about yourself and what you think you deserve. This type of punishment is called shaming. This punishment can feel natural and even good because these negative emotions activate the reward center of your brain. (See Chapter one) The difference between guilt and shame is vital to note. Though often linked together to form what is known as the guilt/shame cycle, there is a clear distinction between the two. Guilt is about what you have done, and shame is about who you are. Guilt can be informative and helpful when it allows us to see a behavior that doesn't match our values or desires. We can use it to decide to make amends and choose to behave differently going forward. However, *being guilty* is an identity, a problem that contributes to deeper issues such as shame. Swallowed guilt becomes shame over time when we connect what we did to who we are. Shame is more deep-rooted and often goes undetected. Shame is a massive grey blanket covering all our experiences, which doesn't allow true feelings through. Author and research professor at the University of Houston, Brene Brown writes this about shame:

Swallowed guilt becomes shame over time when we connect what we did to who we are.

"It can be from one single experience of shame that we are left feeling unlovable. Shame is pervasive throughout our experience—not just limited to the shaming experience. Shame is highly personal—and unique to you based on what you learned from your family and culture growing up. We don't want to talk about it. Left unspoken, shame is very dangerous. Shame cannot survive when brought into the light —it only works in the dark when we feel alone and unable to talk about it. Contagious and hard ... we cannot hear someone else's shame without feeling our own shame and then wanting to avoid it and that person. It is important to know the difference between shame and guilt. Guilt is a focus on behavior and shame a focus on self. Shame is hard to talk about—and so it is avoided. Shame is so painful you want to get out of it. Shame and addiction are closely connected.

Shame is the fear of disconnection—it's the fear that something we've done or failed to do, an ideal that we've not lived up to, or a goal that we've not accomplished makes us unworthy of connection. "I'm not worthy or good enough for love, belonging, or connection. I'm unlovable. I don't belong."

Shame is highly correlated with addiction, violence, aggression, depression, eating disorders, and bullying. And, despite our cultural habit of using shame as punishment, there are NO data to support that shame is a helpful compass for good behavior. In fact, shame is much more likely to be the cause of destructive and hurtful behaviors than it is to be the solution. Secrecy, silence and judgment—shame grows best in this environment—but doused with empathy, shame cannot grow."

She goes on to discuss the power of empathy as the necessary countermeasure against shame. While shame isolates us, empathy offers understanding and connections along with the ability to see oneself as worthwhile and valuable. The *getting over* process is about showing compassion to yourself. To allow the observation and expression of our "it" is a true act of empathy.

It is so painful to live under the shame blanket, yet people do almost anything not to disrupt or get out from under it. The thought, though not necessarily conscious, goes, "if I don't see it, I won't have to feel it." This is also the reason so many living under shame reach for relief through a substance or a relationship in an attempt to numb the pain without having to feel the shame. Again, avoiding what you feel is impossible, and it creates more issues than the shame itself. It becomes the lens through which we see everything.

Denying the validity of our feelings or experiences is one way we can feel shame. It says, "I am wrong for feeling this, and I am bad for having had that experience." The message we send diminishes the experience and creates blame and shame. We make a step to eliminate shame when we give ourselves grace and empathy for our "it" and allow the feelings to exist. Remember, you are not the only one with these experiences. You are valuable, and your feelings matter. These truths help illuminate the truth and diminish the darkness of shame. Most importantly, we read God's message about shame for those in Christ:

"Therefore, **there is now no condemnation** for those who are in Christ Jesus," Romans 8:1

Here's a look at the OVER process applied to guilt and shame:

O - Something happened to me, and I assumed it was my fault, that I am bad.

V - I feel shame about what happened, and that makes sense. I make sense.

E - I will choose to separate what happened to me from who I am.

R - Release the shame, respond in the truth that God does not see you or leave you in shame. Respond and rebuild.

FOURTEEN

OVER: Marriage...

"A great marriage is not when the 'perfect couple' comes together.
It is when an imperfect couple learns to enjoy their differences."
— *Dave Meurer*

If I were to use the three little words, "get over it" in total frustration and a desire for distance, it would be related to the relationship of marriage. I admit on more than one occasion I thought it, but refrained from saying it. Marriage is the most beautiful, closest human relationship we can ever have, sharing life and love forever. However, it is also difficult to be happy and enjoy one another day in and day out. We get stuck in a marriage rut quickly once the "I dos" have been said. Talk about needing a lift out of the grooves in the broken records! I have seen couples who sincerely love one another and want the marriage to work. However, they keep doing what doesn't work and hurting one another, though that's not their intention. They get stuck in a bad loop and don't know how to get out. The loop can become so toxic it can obliterate the relationship.

Many married couples come to therapy frustrated after hearing from their spouse, "Just get over your issues already." The translation is, "I'm tired of hearing about this," and "You are being silly," or "Your feelings are unimportant," or "I just don't want to deal with them any longer." How likely are you to feel better when you hear those words? In a marriage, "get over it" is probably not helpful unless uttered in a better, more positive way.

One of the primary responsibilities of a marriage therapist is to paint a picture of objectivity. The image should be hopeful, a picture of what can be. It is tough to see anything but our "stuff" when we are in the midst of it so the therapists' perspective of what is possible is vital.

After so many years of thinking, "get over it," I found if expressed the right way, the words *can* help. They can serve as a "kick" to get out of the "stuck cycle loop." It's an interruption of old patterns and habits when given in the right context. If your "it" is a stagnant marriage, I would say to both of you, "Get over it and create the marriage you long for and have always wanted." Please know I hear how this might sound. You may be dealing with deep pain and discouragement in your marriage. When I say, "get over it," I'm using the phrase in its positive form.

There has been at least one common denominator with the couples I've worked with. No matter the issue, one theme I see is a lack of perspective about the problem and a general discouragement about the ability to make any change. I have worked with couples who started in hopelessness, but once they recognized the issues with a bit of objectivity, they properly spoke and evaluated their emotions, and started to move in a positive direction. Your marriage is not too far gone. You can resolve the issues by addressing them honestly and doing the work it takes to move to the other side.

Getting over to enjoy: Partnership, cooperation, friendship, intimacy, understanding, unity, connection and all that God has for your marriage.

You've heard it said that people bring baggage with them into marriage, and it's not the pretty designer luggage. These bags are worn and weary, sometimes bulging at the seams about to break open. We don't want our new spouse to see these bags, so we put on our best dog and pony show. When the contents of the bag start showing up in the marriage, we are often surprised because we were not aware before the "I dos" were exchanged. Little by little, exchange after exchange, the baggage starts to unpack itself in the relationship.

Until we deal with our childhood pain, the hurt interrupts the healing process. Buried baggage creates emotional landmines that blow up in the marriage. Generally, we don't know where landmines are because they are underground. Once there is an unexpected explosion, there is uneasiness and fear about the future.

Until we deal with our childhood pain, the hurt interrupts the healing process.

With each burst, an unmanageable dynamic begins. While the landmine owner experiences guilt and the recipient feels hurt, there is little chance of finding solutions or communicating effectively. We start walking on eggshells. Unfortunately, no matter how carefully we walk, the chances are good that we will hit another landmine. We are tempted to blame our spouse for the disruption. It's easy to find reasons why they are the problem. If we look in our partner's bags, we will find plenty of reasons they need to change. In reality, the reason we are bothered is because our spouse poked in our bag, making us vulnerable. We would rather bury our luggage and theirs. Over time, the relationship is full of hidden baggage ready to explode and self-imposed walls. A relationship in this condition it is not likely to survive, much less to experience healthy growth.

To establish and enjoy a healthy marital relationship, open the bags that are sitting in the middle of the room. Do not ignore the bags or trip over them. Take action to interrupt the stuck cycle. See what options exist.

Here's a look at the OVER process applied to Marriage:

O – Open up the bags you brought in. Observe and objectify—Realize your spouse brought bags too. It is not personal, but it is their history. They don't necessarily mean to hurt you.

V – Vent and Validate. "This behavior hurts me and makes me feel like I did when…" and "I don't like this," and "That makes sense."

E – Examine the options—Ask for what you want and don't assume. Get help in counseling, talk more about issues, and take time for one another. Be involved in a supportive community and/or church group that will encourage your marriage.

R – Respond in Truth—God is in this with us and we can do this with His help.

Case Studies

* Names changed

When I first met **Hannah***, she was hoping for help but felt confident she wouldn't find it. She saw many professionals throughout her life. Now, in her 30s, she was unable to see the light at the end of this very dark tunnel. No previous attempts for help provided any meaningful long-term change. Her pain was palpable; her trauma was the worst I had ever seen. She experienced severe abuse and violation of her body, spirit, and mind. It began early in her childhood and continued well into adulthood. The levels of abuse were unfathomable. She recounted the facts of her story, one event more horrific than the last, with a cool detachment. The detachment was her protection from the trauma, to speak it with no emotion as if it did not exist. She spoke as if she was no longer able to hold any optimism about her future. In a sense, she accepted the trauma as her life and a part of her without knowing how to handle any of it. In reality, the deeper attachment to her past became her core, her identity. She spoke about it but did not feel it or separate from it. She wore it and owned it and it overwhelmed her mind and her body. She lived moment to moment, barely able to get through the day without severe panic. Her body told "on" her with multiple medical issues. She experienced absolute terror in response to even the idea of looking objectively at her experiences. She feared it would never get better. It was too painful to look at her experiences outside of herself, but that was the necessary step to create true distance and allow healing. The fear of looking at it was more than she could bear. Though destructive, her ability to find comfort in the familiarity of "coping" seemed a better choice than opening up the possibility of having to relive the pain.

Through many months of working with Hannah, she cycled through the four steps many times. The first step was the sticking point. For survival, she became a survivor, which became her total identity. Everything in life was about what happened to her—she survived the tremendous fear and anxiety caused by the trauma, she got through the day while hiding from the fears. She resisted any logical or cognitive approach to help find healing. She wanted to believe she could move past it, but Hannah needed new tools and someone to remind her that she could do it.

To make any forward movement, I needed to see her not as a patient, but as a person. She so closely identified with what happened to her and what it made her as a result. She had no sense of who she was as a person aside from the trauma and her survivor identity. The breakthrough came when she trusted herself enough and realized she could take off the jersey/mantle of her childhood. Figuratively, she put everything on the table and looked at it as what she experienced, not as what defined her. After this excruciating step, she began to allow the expression and validation of her feelings of trauma. It was in the distance between what happened to her and who she is and wanted to be that she was finally able to break free. She realized she had the power to choose, to weigh her options, and to make choices through the filter of freedom and no longer only survival. Today Hannah is in touch with the strength that was always in her and using it to create a life for herself. Despite difficult memories and grief over her past, she is living with much more peace and joy. She regularly ministers to others and lives in the freedom Christ came to give her. She is well into the process of *getting over*. She recently told me, "God just continues to give me a life filled with transformative joy and redemption everywhere I turn. I finally reached my breakthrough." She is well into the process of *getting over*.

Lydia* grew up in a home where emotions were not present or easily accessed. The daughter of very religious parents, she understood early on that there was a right way and a wrong way for everything. Usually, expressed emotions were considered wrong, even sinful. She experienced sexual violation as a young girl, and when she reported it to her parents, they had little to no response, which made her feel she should also avoid a reaction. From that moment on, she learned to betray her own emotions. Her father tragically died when she was young, and she became the surrogate parent as she took on much of the responsibility for her mother and other siblings. She became the dutiful daughter and sister but felt extraordinarily resentful and bitter. She tucked her feelings away or responded with denial, avoidance, and self-loathing. By the time she came to see me in her 40s, she was a shell of herself, living out of obligation and habit, with very little hope and even less motivation to look for any. She believed that she was not lovable. She looked for every relationship to disappoint her, and she was very reluctant to trust. She was stuck for so long she did not believe it could ever change. Her hard-protective shell left her feeling alone. It took quite a bit of time to gain her trust and make any headway. She had strength that she was not aware of and a tender heart that longed for help which gave her the motivation to continue. The breakthrough came when she objectified her experiences and validated her feelings. Though it was difficult to process this new information against the longstanding belief system she had from childhood, she began to work the *getting over* process. She became aware of the growth and the freedom that came with having and exercising options for herself. She has broken out of the shell and is living authentically for the first time in her life. She has responded in God's Truth and no longer lives under the blanket of shame. Even on her bad days, she understands the struggle and sees it as an opportunity to continue in her growth journey.

Talia* learned early on not to think for herself, or to have her own feelings. She could only choose what agreed with her mother's wishes. She was emotionally and mentally traumatized by her parents. They told her she was mentally disabled and would be unable to pursue any of her dreams and that she was incapable of being on her own. Her mother exhibited extremely narcissistic behavior. She required her daughter to agree and sing her praises in the face of harsh and abusive behavior. Her father was passive and allowed his wife to dominate and dictate in the home. Talia came to me at the request of her mother, who wanted certain behaviors diminished or extinguished. As expected, her behaviors were symptoms of a much greater issue.

As we spent time together, it became apparent that the goal would be to help her find the strength to become independent. Since she was 20 years old, we were able to operate separately from her mother and began work on her goals and desires. It was a very long and challenging path for her because she was still living at home and continued to hear the familiar, negative messages. It took many sessions of speaking her truth and God's truth before she was able to take the first steps toward her healing and freedom. For the first time, she was able to accept that God truly loves her, to feel His love, and to know He has a plan for her life. She learned that she is a person separate from her family and that she matters. She claimed the promise that she "can do all things through Christ who strengthens." She started her over journey by opening up about her "it" and seeing it for what it was. Her difficult, abusive childhood was not her fault. Her parents' behavior was not a reflection of her or who she was. She was able to create distance from that faulty belief to the truth. She learned to state what happened—get it out—then vent and validate the feelings she had in response to those experiences without dismissing or diminishing the impact. She actively chose to move out and start to stand on her own, believing the truth and no longer believing the lies she heard all her life. Today she is living independently, paying her way through college and seeing possibilities for the first time in her life. Though she still has difficult days, she has a framework for moving on and some new experiences of success in using it.

Sam* came to me because he had anxiety and did not understand the cause. He was raised in an upper-class home with a loving family. His father was an alcoholic though it wasn't acknowledged. His mother did all she could do to cover for him and made sure the kids had a good impression of him. He was the conduit for all the relationships in the home. His father spent much of his life hiding the drinking and manipulating those around him so they would not see it—a familiar trait with addicts. The kids learned not to trust themselves or their feelings because what they saw and felt, even in plain sight, was deemed inaccurate. When the parents' marriage of more than 30 years broke up as a result of the father's infidelity, Sam's anxiety accelerated. The rest of the family responded with denial and swept the affair and divorce under the rug to "get along and make peace," rather than deal with the truth and experience any conflict. He felt pressure to do the same but was tired of pretending. His anxiety was a result of his many years of swallowing emotions and discounting them. He realized in his family feelings were either completely ignored or expressed in an out of control, scary way.

The first step was big for Sam when he understood his feelings were just feelings, neither right or wrong. He couldn't comprehend this concept. It was as if I was speaking in a different language to him. He gained insight when he made the distinction between the emotion and the expression of the feelings. When he acknowledged his pain, he began to heal. He gained hope when he realized his feelings were not wrong, and he could control them. He identified his "it" and worked backward. When he acknowledged the anger and anxiety, he saw the origin and chose what to do with the now validated feelings. He is working the *getting over* process to help create healthy boundaries with his family, and to give himself permission to move forward and choose next steps.

Richard* struggled to move past the experiences of his childhood that disrupted his sense of identity early on. His mother left him when he was only 12 years old, and his father's remarriage intensified his sense of despair because his new step-mother was also dismissive of him. It was a classic Cinderella story, but in this case, the trauma of his mother abandoning him was more devastating than the "evil" step-mother storyline. At a young age, he sometimes had to fend for himself with no resources because his father focused on the new wife's happiness, at the expense of his son's needs. No one helped him to process his feelings, and the adults in his life acted as if nothing was wrong. He identified as reject-able and unlovable. He chose his relationships on these criteria, which led to an unsuccessful marriage and broken relationships after that. He had a misconstrued view of women based on his previous experience with the important women in his childhood. He was stuck because he had empathy and faith that told him to forgive, so he ignored or denied his own emotions as he moved toward that faithful step of forgiveness, thereby keeping the false identity in place. He was reluctant to see his mother and his father because they represented a threat to his understanding. Therefore, he was unable remove the "family jersey."

Now in his late 40s, he still struggles to feel valuable, to allow himself to see past who he thought he was, to who God says he is. Though he knows of God's love in His head and is a Christ-follower, he can't seem to separate his childhood experience from his current reality—extremely successful as a parent and in his career. It was a hard first step for Richard to acknowledge his parents failed him. This realization threatened his need to see them as good, which meant he felt he was wrong, and the reason behind their failure. He continues to work the *getting over* process to allow for the feelings to point him to the "it" that happened to him. In this case, the "it" is abandonment and neglect, which led him to operate with an extreme need to control, which led to broken relationships and a sense of shame. His ability to accept their shortcomings and his feelings in response validated him and relieved him of the weight he had been carrying. He is finally living the life he would never allow himself even to dream possible, and enjoying himself as he looks to the next phase of life.

When Maria* walked into my office, I was immediately impressed with her self-assured and calm demeanor. She was a professional in a very competitive, male-dominated field and had achieved a high level of success at a young age. She came to counseling at the request of her current boyfriend, Javier*, who I previously saw one-on-one. He asked if she could join the session because they were having issues in their relationship. Quickly, it became clear that he wanted me to agree that what she said and did was the source of their relationship trouble. As a rule, I always assume a neutral position in working with couples and know that the truth lies somewhere between their two reports. I was interested to hear from her, and as expected, her side of the story was different than his. The relationship started in a fairy tale fashion. He was in awe of her talent, strength, and beauty. He was also intimidated by these qualities. She believed he would be the one to "break the curse." Soon after establishing they were dating, things shifted. His admiration became resentment, and to attempt to curb his intimidation, he tried to dominate her.

My initial assessment of a calm, self-assured Maria was true of her character and in her professional life, but not in her relationship with Javier. Over the next few months of therapy, I saw her change from self-assured to insecure, from carefree to conflicted. She became a shell of herself in her attempt to prove that she was worthy and deserving of his attention. She was willing to endure abject mental and verbal abuse as the relationship devolved. He played with her emotions as a cat plays with a mouse, pouncing, and then letting up to see if the game was still on. He continued this behavior while slowly extinguishing the life out of her. It was as if she believed that any scrap from his table was better than nothing. He was less interested in therapy as time went on, and he refused to acknowledge any challenges to his behavior. He soon dropped out, and she continued. We started to explore the why behind her behavior, and that's when I realized she was stuck. Everyone could say they've had a bad relationship, but in Maria's case, it was the same relationship experience repeatedly, like a broken record. She played that record since childhood. It all started with the relationship she saw her mother and father have, particularly the one she had with her father.

Maria learned early on in her life that it was her job to prove herself as acceptable to her father. He was not around very much, and when he was, she was desperate for his attention and love. Sometimes, despite her best efforts to please him, he blatantly rejected her and told her to "go away." For days after, he didn't make eye contact with her, and he treated he as if she did not exist. Her mother was unable or unwilling to intervene, which cemented the message she received: "You are reject-able. You must please everyone. You are not to think of yourself."

She stood on these foundational "it" bricks and functioned from that vantage point. She had at least three relationships before Javier and were all the same. She subjugated herself, her career, her intelligence, her needs, and her bank account to serve the man in her life, only to be rejected and humiliated. She continued to pick the "same man" in an attempt to heal the relationship wound that originated with her father. When she arrived at a low point in the relationship, she didn't have the strength to end it due to her deep desire to be accepted. The pain of being in an extremely unhealthy relationship was not worse than the pain of her validated wound. She stayed for years at a time, long after she knew the relationship was over.

Eventually, Maria was able to move past Javier but continued to replay the relationship record for another six years. She made small gains with each relationship—finding less harmful ones, but it wasn't until we started to use the *getting over* process, that she was able to think clearly and begin to make meaningful gains in healing from her past.

Today, she is actively working the steps and realizes how powerful the childhood experience was as an imprint for all future relationships. (She also struggled to have any boundaries with friendships and her employees). The ability to identify, understand, and objectify the "it" that had been a barrier to healthy relationships allowed her to validate her feelings and make new choices about what she wanted for herself. She is making progress and realizing her value, which in turn requires others around her to do the same. She is no longer stuck!

Appendices

Stuck Quotient Assessment

Are you STUCK?

Answer these questions about the "it" you are trying to Get OVER to find your Stuck Quotient (SQ):

- Do you know something is blocking your happiness or success but can't identify it?

- Are you frustrated with multiple failed attempts to find a solution?

- Do you often feel angry about? Is your anger misplaced?

- Do you blame yourself or others for the problems you experience?

- Do you think you just have to "cope with it?"

- Do you think you are the only one with this problem?

- Do you feel guilty or ashamed?

- Do you think your feelings are inappropriate or wrong?

- Has anyone told you to "get over it already?"

- Are you repeating behaviors that have not worked in the past?

- Have you lost hope that it can be resolved?

- Do you deny it is a barrier in your current functioning and relationships?

- Do you try to avoid confronting it?

- Do you try to live "around" the issue?

- Do your relationships suffer as a result?

*Take the free quiz and get your SQ online at **thegetoveritbook.com***

Scripture Found in the Book

"A thief is only there to steal and kill and destroy. I came so they can have real and eternal life, more and better life than they ever dreamed of." - John 10:10 (MSG)

"For God has not given us the spirit of fear; but of power, and of love, and of a sound mind." - 2 Timothy 1:7 (KJV)

"So if the Son sets you free, you will be free indeed." - John 8:36 (NIV)

"Unless the Lord builds the house, the builders labor in vain.
Unless the Lord watches over the city, the guards stand watch in vain.
² In vain you rise early and stay up late,

toiling for food to eat—for he grants sleep to[a] those he loves." - Psalm 127 (NIV).

127 [1-2] "If God doesn't build the house, the builders only build shacks.
If God doesn't guard the city, the night watchman might as well nap.
It's useless to rise early and go to bed late, and work your worried fingers to the bone.
Don't you know he enjoys giving rest to those he loves?" - Psalm 127 (MSG)

"Be ye angry, and sin not: let not the sun go down upon your wrath." - Ephesians 4:26 (ASV)

"Go ahead and be angry. You do well to be angry—but don't use your anger as fuel for revenge. And don't stay angry. Don't go to bed angry. Don't give the Devil that kind of foothold in your life." - Ephesians 4:26-27 (MSG)

"Faithful are the wounds of a friend…profuse are the kisses of an enemy". - Proverbs 27:6 (ESV),

"and let us consider how we may spur one another on toward love and good deeds." - Hebrews 10:24 (NIV)

"…in this godless world you will continue to experience difficulties…" - John 16:33 (NIV)

"Do not conform to the pattern of this world, but be transformed by the renewing of your mind. Then you will be able to test and approve what God's will is—his good, pleasing and perfect will." - Romans 12:2 (NIV)

"Do not remember the former things, Nor consider the things of old. Behold, I will do a new thing. Now it shall spring forth; Shall you not know it? I will even make a road in the wilderness, And rivers in the desert." - Isaiah 43:18-19 (NKJV),

"This is what God says,
the God who builds a road right through the ocean,
who carves a path through pounding waves,
The God who summons horses and chariots and armies—
they lie down and then can't get up;
they're snuffed out like so many candles:
"Forget about what's happened;
don't keep going over old history.
Be alert, be present. I'm about to do something brand-new.
It's bursting out! Don't you see it?
There it is! I'm making a road through the desert,
rivers in the badlands.
Wild animals will say 'Thank you!'
—the coyotes and the buzzards—
Because I provided water in the desert,
rivers through the sun-baked earth,
Drinking water for the people I chose,
the people I made especially for myself,
a people custom-made to praise me."
Isaiah 43:18-19 (MSG)

"Trust God from the bottom of your heart;
don't try to figure out everything on your own.
Listen for God's voice in everything you do, everywhere you go;
he's the one who will keep you on track."
Proverbs 3:5-6 (MSG)

"**Open up** before God, keep nothing back, He'll do whatever needs to be done. He'll validate your life in the clear light of day and stamp you with approval at high noon" - Psalm 37:5 (MSG)

"Open your mouth and taste, open your eyes and see—how good God is. Blessed are you who run to Him." - Psalm 34:8 (MSG)

"Then you will know the truth, and the truth will set you free." - John 8:32 (NIV)
Psalm 37:5 (NIV)

"…in all these things we are more than conquerors through him who loved us." - Romans 8:37 (NIV)

"But you are a chosen people, a royal priesthood, a holy nation, God's special possession, that you may declare the praises of him who called you out of darkness into his wonderful light." - 1 Peter 2:9 (NIV)

"For we are God's handiwork, created in Christ Jesus to do good works, which God prepared in advance for us to do." - Ephesians 2:10 (NIV)

"Now if we are children, then we are heirs- heirs of God and co-heirs with Christ. If indeed we share in His sufferings in order that we may also share with His glory." - Romans 8:17 (NIV)

"What a God we have! And how fortunate we are to have him, this Father of our Master Jesus! Because Jesus was raised from the dead, we've been given a brand-new life and have everything to live for, including a future in heaven - and the future starts now!" - 1 Peter 1:3-4 MSG

"Oh yes, you shaped me first inside, then out; you formed me in my mother's womb. I thank you, High God—you're breathtaking! Body and soul, I am marvelously made! I worship in adoration—what a creation! You know me inside and out, you know every bone in my body; You know exactly how I was made, bit by bit, how I was sculpted from nothing into something. Like an open book, you watched me grow from conception to birth; all the stages of my life were spread out before you. The days of my life all prepared before I'd even lived one day." - Psalm 139:13-16 (MSG)

"So, what do you think? With God on our side like this, how can we lose? If God didn't hesitate to put everything on the line for us, embracing our condition and exposing himself to the worst by sending his own Son, is there anything else he wouldn't gladly and freely do for us? And who would dare tangle with God by messing with one of God's chosen? Who would dare even to point a finger? The One who died for us—who was raised to life for us!—is in the presence of God at this very moment sticking up for us. Do you think anyone is going to be able to drive a wedge between us and Christ's love for us? There is no way! Not trouble, not hard times, not hatred, not hunger, not homelessness, not bullying threats, not backstabbing, not even the worst sins listed in Scripture:

They kill us in cold blood because they hate you. We're sitting ducks; they pick us off one by one. None of this fazes us because Jesus loves us. I'm absolutely convinced that nothing—nothing living or dead, angelic or demonic, today or tomorrow, high or low, thinkable or unthinkable—absolutely nothing can get between us and God's love because of the way that Jesus our Master has embraced us." - Romans 8:31-39 The Message (MSG)

"This resurrection life you received from God is not a timid, grave-tending life. It's adventurously expectant, greeting God with a childlike "What's next, Papa?" God's Spirit touches our spirits and confirms who we really are. We know who he is, and we know who we are: Father and children. And we know we are going to get what's coming to us—an unbelievable inheritance! We go through exactly what Christ goes through. If we go through the hard times with him, then we're certainly going to go through the good times with him!" - Romans 8:15-17 (MSG)

"We had dreams," they said to him, "but there is no one to interpret them. Then Joseph said to them, "Don't interpretations belong to God? Tell me your dreams." - Genesis 40:8 (HCSB)

"If it is possible, as far as it depends on you, live at peace with everyone." - Romans 12:18 (NIV)

"Do not take revenge, my dear friends, but leave room for God's wrath, for it is written: "It is mine to avenge; I will repay," says the Lord. [20] On the contrary: "If your enemy is hungry, feed him; if he is thirsty, give him something to drink. In doing this, you will heap burning coals on his head. Do not be overcome by evil, but overcome evil with good." - Romans 8:19-21 (NIV)

"But there is another urgency before me now. I feel compelled to go to Jerusalem. I'm completely in the dark about what will happen when I get there. I do know that it won't be any picnic, for the Holy Spirit has let me know repeatedly and clearly that there are hard times and imprisonment ahead. But that matters little. What matters most to me is to finish what God started: the job the Master Jesus gave me of letting everyone I meet know all about this incredibly extravagant generosity of God." - Acts 20:22-24 (MSG)

"So how am I to respond? I've decided that I really don't care about their motives, whether mixed, bad, or indifferent. Every time one of them opens his mouth, Christ is proclaimed, so I just cheer them on!

And I'm going to keep that celebration going because I know how it's going to turn out. Through your faithful prayers and the generous response of the Spirit of Jesus Christ, everything he wants to do in and through me will be done. I can hardly wait to continue on my course. I don't expect to be embarrassed in the least. On the contrary, everything happening to me in this jail only serves to make Christ more accurately known, regardless of whether I live or die. They didn't shut me up; they gave me a pulpit! Alive, I'm Christ's messenger; dead, I'm his bounty. Life versus even more life! I can't lose." - Philippians 1:18-21 (MSG)

"God is able to orchestrate everything to work toward something good and beautiful when we love him and accept his invitation to live according to his plan." - Romans 8:28 (THE VOICE)

"Do not conform to the pattern of this world, but be transformed by the **renewing** of your mind. Then you will be able to test and approve what God's will is—his good, pleasing and perfect will." - Romans 12:2 (NIV)

"Not that I have already obtained this or am already perfect, but I press on to make it my own, because Christ Jesus has made me his own. Brothers, I do not consider that I have made it my own. But one thing I do: forgetting what lies behind and straining forward to what lies ahead, I press on toward the goal for the prize of the upward call of God in Christ Jesus." - Philippians 3:12-14 (NIV)

Place Your Life Before God

"So here's what I want you to do, God helping you: Take your everyday, ordinary life—your sleeping, eating, going-to-work, and walking-around life—and place it before God as an offering. Embracing what God does for you is the best thing you can do for him. Don't become so well-adjusted to your culture that you fit into it without even thinking. Instead, fix your attention on God. You'll be changed from the inside out. Readily recognize what he wants from you, and quickly respond to it. Unlike the culture around you, always dragging you down to its level of immaturity, God brings the best out of you, develops well-formed maturity in you." - Romans 12:2 (MSG)

"We demolish arguments and every pretension that sets itself up against the knowledge of God, and we take captive every thought to make it obedient to Christ." - 2 Corinthians 10:5 (NIV)

"If you ask (demand) anything in my name, I will do it" - John 14:14

"The tested genuineness of your faith – more precious than gold that perishes though it is tested by fire may result in praise and glory and honor at the revelation of Jesus Christ" - 1 Peter 1:7 (ESV)

"Then I will (restore) make up to you for the years that the swarming locust has eaten, The creeping locust, the stripping locust and the gnawing locust, My great army which I sent among you." - Joel 2:25 NASB

"Most assuredly, I say to you, he who believes in me, the works that I do will he do also; and greater works than these he will do, because I go to the Father" (John 14:12).

"Therefore God exalted him to the highest place
and gave him the name that is above every name,
[10] that at the name of Jesus every knee should bow,
in heaven and on earth and under the earth,
[11] and every tongue acknowledge that Jesus Christ is Lord,
to the glory of God the Father." – Philippians 2:9-11

"But they overcame him by the blood of the Lamb and by the word of their testimony, and they did not love their lives so much that they were afraid to die," Rev. 12:11 (NET)

"No, in all these things we are more than conquerors through him who loved us." - Romans 8:3 (NIV))

"For not one of us lives for himself, and not one dies for himself; [8] for if we live, we live for the Lord, or if we die, we die for the Lord; therefore whether we live or die, we are the Lord's." - Romans 14:7-9 (NASB)

"All praise to the God and Father of our Master, Jesus the Messiah! Father of all mercy! God of all healing counsel! He comes alongside us when we go through hard times, and before you know it, he brings us alongside someone else who is going through hard times so that we can be there for that person just as God was there for us. We have plenty of hard times that come from following the Messiah, but no more so than the good times of his healing comfort—we get a full measure of that, too." - 2 Corinthians 1:3-5 (MSG)

"But we do not belong to those who shrink back and are destroyed, but to those who have faith and are saved." - Hebrews 10:39 (NIV)

"You make known to me the path of life; In your presence there is fullness of joy, in your right hand are pleasures for evermore" - Psalm 16:11 (ESV)

"You shall eat in plenty and be satisfied, and praise the name of the Lord your God, who has dealt wondrously with you. And my people shall never again be put to shame. You shall know that I am in the midst of Israel, and that I am the LORD your God and there is none else. And my people shall never again be put to shame" - Joel 2:26-27 (NRSV)

"So let's do it—full of belief, confident that we're present-able inside and out. Let's keep a firm grip on the promises that keep us going. He always keeps his word. Let's see how inventive we can be in encouraging love and helping out, not avoiding worshiping together as some do but spurring each other on, especially as we see the big Day approaching". - Hebrews 10:22-25 The Message (MSG)

"The Spirit of God, the Master, is on me because God anointed me. He sent me to preach good news to the poor, heal the heartbroken, Announce freedom to all captives, pardon all prisoners." - Isaiah 61:1 (NIV)

"The Spirit of the Sovereign Lord is on me,
because the Lord has anointed me
to proclaim good news to the poor.

He has sent me to bind up the brokenhearted,
to proclaim freedom for the captives
and release from darkness for the prisoners

It is for freedom that Christ has set us free. Stand firm,
then, and do not let yourselves be burdened again by a yoke
of slavery." - Galatians - 5:1 (NIV)

"I can do ALL THINGS through Christ who strengthens
me." - Philippians 4:13 (NIV)

"This is how much God loved the world: He gave his Son,
his one and only Son. And this is why: so that no one need
be destroyed; by believing in him, anyone can have a whole
and lasting life." - John 3:16 (MSG)

"Christ arrives right on time to make this happen. He
didn't, and doesn't, wait for us to get ready. He presented
himself for this sacrificial death when we were far too weak
and rebellious to do anything to get ourselves ready. And
even if we hadn't been so weak, we wouldn't have known
what to do anyway". - Romans 5:8 (MSG)

"With the arrival of Jesus, the Messiah, that fateful
dilemma is resolved. Those who enter into Christ's being-
here-for-us no longer have to live under a continuous,
low-lying black cloud." - Romans 8:1-7 (MSG)

One of my favorite songs is from Elevation Worship. It speaks of the walls that we face, and of the God who is faithful to meet us in and help us break through those hard places. It always brings me comfort to refocus on the God of the Promise and where my confidence rests. When I feel stuck or discouraged, this is my anthem! I think it might help you as well. I encourage you to listen to it, but in the meantime, here are the words:

"Do It Again"

Walking around these walls
I thought by now they'd fall
But You have never failed me yet
Waiting for change to come
Knowing the battle's won
For You have never failed me yet

Your promise still stands
Great is Your faithfulness, faithfulness
I'm still in Your hands
This is my confidence, You've never failed me yet

I know the night won't last
Your Word will come to pass
My heart will sing Your praise again
Jesus You're still enough
Keep me within Your love
My heart will sing Your praise again

Your promise still stands
Great is Your faithfulness, faithfulness
I'm still in Your hands
This is my confidence, You never failed

I've seen You move, You move the mountains
And I believe, I'll see You do it again
You made a way, where there was no way
And I believe, I'll see You do it again

Written by <u>Chris Brown</u>, Mack Brock, Matt Redman, Steven Furtick
Produced by <u>Aaron Robertson</u> & <u>Mack Brock</u>
Album: <u>There Is a Cloud</u>, 2009, Elevation Worship Publishing (BMI)
Printed with permission

Feelings Chart

For those needing a little help with feelings...

Pleasant Feelings

OPEN	HAPPY	ALIVE	GOOD
understanding	great	playful	calm
confident	gay	courageous	peaceful
reliable	joyous	energetic	at ease
easy	lucky	liberated	comfortable
amazed	fortunate	optimistic	pleased
free	delighted	provocative	encouraged
sympathetic	overjoyed	impulsive	clever
interested	gleeful	free	surprised

satisfied	thankful	frisky	content
receptive	important	animated	quiet
accepting	festive	spirited	certain
kind	ecstatic	thrilled	relaxed
	satisfied	wonderful	serene
	glad		free and easy
	cheerful		bright
	sunny		blessed
	merry		reassured
	elated		
	Jubilant		

LOVE	INTERESTED	POSITIVE	STRONG
loving	concerned	eager	impulsive
considerate	affected	keen	free
affectionate	fascinated	earnest	sure
sensitive	intrigued	intent	certain
tender	absorbed	anxious	rebellious
devoted	inquisitive	inspired	unique
attracted	nosy	determined	dynamic
passionate	snoopy	excited	tenacious
admiration	engrossed	enthusiastic	hardy
warm	curious	bold	secure
touched		brave	
sympathy		daring	
close		challenged	
loved		optimistic	

comforted		re-enforced	
drawn toward		confident	
		hopeful	
Difficult/ Unpleasant Feelings			
ANGRY	**DEPRESSED**	**CONFUSED**	**HELPLESS**
irritated	lousy	upset	incapable
enraged	disappointed	doubtful	alone
hostile	discouraged	uncertain	paralyzed
insulting	ashamed	indecisive	fatigued
sore	powerless	perplexed	useless
annoyed	diminished	embarrassed	inferior
upset	guilty	hesitant	vulnerable
hateful	dissatisfied	shy	empty
unpleasant	miserable	stupefied	forced
offensive	detestable	disillusioned	hesitant
bitter	repugnant	unbelieving	despair
aggressive	despicable	skeptical	frustrated
resentful	disgusting	distrustful	distressed
inflamed	abominable	misgiving	woeful
provoked	terrible	lost	pathetic
incensed	in despair	unsure	tragic
infuriated	sulky	uneasy	in a stew
cross	bad	pessimistic	dominated
worked up	a sense of loss	tense	

boiling			
fuming			
Indignant			
INDIFFERENT	**AFRAID**	**HURT**	**SAD**
insensitive	fearful	crushed	tearful
dull	terrified	tormented	sorrowful
nonchalant	suspicious	deprived	pained
neutral	anxious	pained	grief
reserved	alarmed	tortured	anguish
weary	panic	dejected	desolate
bored	nervous	rejected	desperate
preoccupied	scared	injured	pessimistic
cold	worried	offended	unhappy
disinterested	frightened	afflicted	lonely
lifeless	timid	aching	grieved
	shaky	victimized	mournful
	restless	heartbroken	dismayed
	doubtful	agonized	
	threatened	appalled	
	cowardly	humiliated	
	quaking	wronged	
	menaced	alienated	
	wary		

About the Author

Sally Livingston has been a Licensed Marriage and Family Therapist and a ministry leader for over 25 years. She is a gifted speaker for marriage and family topics, as well as in the arena of conflict resolution and anger management. She is a team developer and consultant for churches and businesses, a Certified RightPath Trainer, and Prepare/Enrich Facilitator. Sally is passionate about helping people understand the issues in their lives that prevent them from living in freedom and equipping them to make the changes necessary to move past the "stuck" places. Sally and her husband of 28 years, Scott, are blessed with three exceptional adult children, and they currently live in Florida.

GET
OVER
IT!

TAKE YOUR NEXT STEP:

- Take the free STUCK QUOTIENT ASSESSMENT @ THEGETOVERITBOOK.COM

Answer 15 questions to determine your personal SQ (Stuck Quotient) results.

- Enroll in the GET OVER IT! Self Study Course

You've read the book,
now start your own getting OVER process!
This 4-module course offers a practical, step-by-step plan
with worksheets and helpful guidance to take you from
being "stuck" to your breakthrough!

- Work your getting OVER plan one-on-one with Sally.

Let her lead you through a transformational process past
your pain and frustration toward freedom from your "it."

FIND OUT MORE AT
THEGETOVERITBOOK.COM

BRING SALLY INTO YOUR CHURCH OR ORGANIZATION

LICENSED MARRIAGE AND FAMILY THERAPIST. AUTHOR. SPEAKER. TRAINER. CONSULTANT.

Sally knows the importance of choosing the right person for the job. It can mean the difference between a meaningful event and a waste of time and resources. Sally's authentic and caring approach combined with her therapy and ministry experience uniquely positions her as the right person for the job. She customizes each message and training session to achieve and exceed the objectives of her clients.

CONTACT SALLY TODAY TO BEGIN THE CONVERSATION
SallyLivingston.com

TESTIMONIALS

"Sally is a gifted speaker. If you are looking for someone to lead marriage and family events, staff development or care ministry formation, please let me commend her to you."
**Mark Lesher, Executive Pastor,
Christ Journey Church**

"Sally has a poised approach which brings confidence to any group she partners with. She makes organizations and relationships stronger."
Lilibeth Garcia, Founder, The Legacy Ministries

"Sally brought my wife and I 'home'. The tools she shared with us helped return our relationship to the beautiful, supportive and loving place it had once been."
M & C, married couple

CPSIA information can be obtained
at www.ICGtesting.com
Printed in the USA
FSHW020011011119
63613FS